THE AIKI SINGULARITY

THE AIKI
SINGULARITY

SCOTT MEREDITH

See Otter Books

Published by See Otter Books

ISBN 978-1-5411-2231-4

Typesetting services by BOOKOW.COM

CONTENTS

NOTES

All translations from the Chinese and Japanese are the original work of the author unless otherwise explicitly sourced. Most Chinese characters are traditional, with occasional variation including adoption of simplified characters, based on common usage, personal preference, and accepted historical precedent in names, among other criteria. Most Chinese transliterations are Pinyin, with occasional variation including adoption of Wade-Giles and other variants, based on common usage, personal preference, and accepted historical precedent in names, among other criteria. Artwork concept and design by Scott Meredith. Illustrations by Jeremy Ray unless otherwise specified.

CAUTION

Cast of Characters

Guo Yunshen (1829-1900) Xingyiquan supermaster.

Li Nengran (Luoneng) (1807–1888) Founding supermaster of modern Xingyiquan.

Sagawa Yukiyoshi (1902-1998) Premier martial artist of the 20th century.

Sun Lutang (1860-1933) Internal martial arts supermaster.

Takeda Sokaku (1859-1943) Daito Ryu Aiki Jujutsu supermaster, teacher of Sagawa.

Yang Chengfu (1883-1936) Tai Chi supermaster, grandson of Yang Luchan, founder of modern Tai Chi.

Zhang Sanfeng (Southern Song Dynasty) Legendary creator of Tai Chi.

Zheng Manqing (1902-1975) Tai Chi supermaster, student of Yang Chengfu, and creator of the uniquely soft and profoundly "internal" ZMQ37 Tai Chi form.

INTRODUCTION

There's something *out there*. And it's *in here* too. It has *no religion* – yet it arises from spirit. It has *no culture* – yet it's steeped in Asian mythology. It has *no ideology* – yet charismatic cults have been built atop it. It has *no economy* – yet serious money has been minted from it. It has *no aesthetics* – yet it's often dolled up in stage theatrics, colorful costumes, and cinematic histrionics. It has *no science* – but when you feel it you won't need a weatherman telling you how the wind blows.

It's the universal, ubiquitous power of nature's Great Way. Even the learned philosophers of ancient times couldn't do any better than I just did. They put up their hands and surrendered:

吾不知其名。字之曰道。強爲之名曰大。

I don't know its name. When I must name it, I say only 'the Way'. If forced to describe it, I have only the word 'Great'.

But that kind of philosophical talk is eye-glazing stuff - well known from a thousand and one translations of the ancient Dao De Jing (道德經). And therein lies the problem. People reading that kind of thing assume it's all fluff. Just *words* or *concepts* or *images* or *ideals*. Nothing to see here. Nothing to feel. Nothing to knock your socks clean off.

The trouble with the internal energy teaching business is that everybody treats the topic as a *metaphor*. Or an *image* for meditation. Or a philosophical *concept*. Or just a *word*. It all seems so abstract. Thus, the default reaction when encountering the inner energy verbiage is a yawn.

But the verbiage gives us a starting point: *words*. Words are, after all, formations of air. So am I talking about air? You might think so, because氣, a common Chinese term for internal energy, is usually translated as 'air'. But that would be barking up the wrong *qi*. Air is an ordinary physical phenomenon. But the *something* cited above is radically, seriously something *else*.

Paradoxically, the view of internal power as a mere abstraction stampedes people to the polar opposite error: *material reductionism*. After all (the reasoning goes) even though we can't trust the ancients to have simply said what they meant, still surely they weren't *that* totally nutso. They must have had *something* in mind. So now there are a slew of interpretations of the internal power as a particular type of tissue in the body. Or a certain way of moving or bracing your body as a mechanical structure. All these are equally wrong.

The Tai Chi Classic writings (太極拳經) are a user's manual for a total consciousness blowout and blowup. When you're holding the Classics, or any book on Tai Chi, you should feel respect. As though it's a sheaf of LSD blotter sheets, hundred hits per page. That's how potent this inner technology can be.

Yet over and over, the big existential question *why* resurfaces. Why bother to cultivate this stuff? I have covered that in pedantic detail as 'The Big Picture' (final chapter of my book *Juice Radical Taiji Energetics*). But it's an underlying thread, or atmospheric theme, in all my books: *What's the point?* There are all these methods and drills and protocols, but what is the pot of gold at rainbow's end? After all, I personally don't do combat sports, I don't work as a SWAT commando. I don't have a professional chiropractic concern or run an acupuncture clinic or any other alternative healing practice, so.... WTF man?

If, just by pressing a button or taking a pill, people could instantly feel even 1% of what I'm laying out (the internal result of these methods), the whole motivation thing would never come up. But since so few have any idea of it, I have to keep hinting at the result, dragging in tired marketing hooks: maybe you'll get some little self-defense ability against street punks ... maybe you won't fall as often, or as dangerously ...? Or, maybe it'll lower your blood pressure a couple points... I have to talk in these cloddish ways. Of course, the training can have some of those benefits. Better balance for seniors!

That's the Tai Chi marketing playbook, but I don't care much about any of that. I'm not really suited, in the standard sense, to be a professional teacher of this stuff. A real teacher in the modern world is first and foremost a marketer who should be able to sell iceboxes to Eskimos. Smile as you kill. Subprime mortgages. Always Be Closing... that kind of mentality. (I *can* be very cheesy, but not in that particular way.)

But I'll end run the whole question with this: **Nobody ever asks about the 'motivation' for sex, drugs and rock n roll.** *You just don't ask that!* And why not? Because you'd look stupid. The motivation is self-evident: they are amazing, thrilling, spectacular, super-cool *experiences*. They are the three self-justifying activities. And now the fourth: Tai Chi.

Anybody could say exactly what I've said here about their own little hobby. They like it because it's fun. Mountain climbing, white water rafting, surf fishing, yoga, squirrel-suit para-flying - whatever. But at the end of the day, *everybody* has to admit that Sex, Drugs, and Rock 'n Roll... those three are in a class by themselves. Nobody asks 'why' in the moment of eating, sleeping having sex, etc. We just 'do it' because we want to, it feels good then and there. No deep philosophical or practical rationale has any relevance. There may be some genetic or evolutionary dispensation for any given behavior (heath, attractiveness, social bonding, reproduction, protection... in a nutshell: *inclusive fitness*). But in the moment that stuff doesn't matter. You'll come to feel the same way about the *why* of your internal practice.

But because this internal stuff is hard to kick-start, grinding as it does against the grain of our relentless physicality, I still have to serve up lame little justifications like every other teacher out there. But my heart's not truly in that game. Anybody who wonders *why* just isn't sufficiently *experienced* yet. I don't say this with any rancor. I blame myself, that now, after (how many?) books and DVD's and videos and blog posts and seminars, I still haven't found the optimal way to lay it out more plainly, and make it more accessible.

What do people want from Tai Chi or Qi Gong or from any of the 'personal energy' disciplines? I would list the hoped-for benefits as follows.

- They want to be associated with an attractive, glamorous, cheery, warm, sparkly, protective and comfortable **TEACHER FIGURE**. They want a Santa Claus, a Daddy/Mommy, a figure to whom they can attach emotional cords of (hopefully bilateral) care, affection, meaning, power, and love. This drive to barnacle on to somebody else's (attributed) personal charm is more powerful than any other human motivation.
- They want to feel immediate, straightforward **MEDICAL RESULTS** meaning some slight relief of any chronic physical pain, ache, or other pre-existing medical/health condition. Beyond that, overall greater sprightliness in daily life activities. Of course, there is a lot of placebo effect happening under the hood in this realm.

- They desire a **SOCIAL EXPERIENCE**, the feeling of meaning and safety found in group bonding within a community, common interests, before-and-after small talk, internet chatting, prescribed uniform colors, potluck dinners, etc.

- A small minority holds a fantasy about **COMBATIVE SKILLS** for possible self-defense against PCP-fueled street thug attacks, carjacking, and home invasions. This is a minority of the population though, because most actual hardcore martial athletes and/or law enforcement or professional security types are less likely to get anywhere near traditional internal training in the first place.

- There are those with historical, cultural or **AESTHETIC INTEREST**, appreciation, even reverence for the visual and external performative aspects of these arts. Silk sashes, double fans, monkey jumps, flashing tinfoil swords ... that kind of thing.

That covers the majority of people who ever dip a toe into Tai Chi, Qi Gong, or any martial art that isn't purely sport or law-enforcement/military oriented. While I may sound cold in parsing these out, I'm not disparaging these goals or the people who pursue them. Just like any human activity, they can be fun to chase. But I need to distinguish everything above from what I'm trying to teach with energy-centric Tai Chi.

I teach one thing and one thing alone: *energy and the cultivation of energy.* That's the first justification for the title word: SINGULARITY. If you begin to truly understand, consciously control, and continuously amplify the internal energy, you *will* simultaneously make progress with the peripheral considerations above. But it isn't the same focus, because I care primarily about working the energy of, by, and for itself. I leave to others the possible connections between the energy experience per se (in the raw) vs. the bullet points above.

One other tip: *don't assume you know it.* I've often taught somebody an energetic practice or effect in precise detail, only to realize later that the person merely assimilated it to something they already knew, based on superficial resemblance. For example, the Cat Step Protocol may seem like a general concept you've heard a million times in other Tai Chi teachings, but if you don't work it precisely as specified here, if you just lump it in with Cloud Hands or some other thing that you (think you) already know, you'll miss it by a mile. Later, once you've experienced the various blowout effects for yourself, *then* you can start to vary it and play freely.

The energetic essence of internal power training is straightforward and technical. It is neither spiritual fantasy (on the high end) nor physiological reductionism (on the low end). It's a kind of personal technology that you can apply and experience for yourself.

It amazes me that we spend so much money and time diverting ourselves with movies, video games, drugs, booze, Prozac, religion, gambling, pro sports, shopping, fitness etc. These aren't bad things but they fade like a birthday candle in the vast sunlight of the ARC experience. Only a disciplined mind and a radical soul has any chance of grokking what I'm putting out here. Maybe those are in short supply, but give yourself a chance to find out whether you're one of them.

THE ARC MODEL

I've presented the Accumulate/Rebound/Catch (ARC) model of internal energy flow in all my prior works. Even if you've read those, read this section for review, reinforcement, and elaboration.

The ARC, as both conceptual model and as accessible, tangible experience, is much less complex than the Taoist organ-linking practices and other *neidan* (內丹) internal alchemy theory you may have read or heard about. It's a natural phenomenon and if you understand it you can work with it directly in yourself. Ultimately it's hardly more difficult than learning to dribble a basketball smoothly and make a few trick shots.

But at the start you have to do two crucial things:

1. You must suspend your skepticism and disbelief and bullshit detector and *nobody fools me* mind. You must put that aside long enough to really work this stuff. If you can't do that for a time, forget the whole thing right now.

2. You must follow directions precisely in the beginning. Don't worry, I'm not oppressing you forever, once you know what you're doing you'll be free as water to do whatever you will.

The essential insight of the ARC was known long ago to the authors of the classical Chinese writings about internal martial arts, such as the Tai Chi Classics (attributed to Zhang Sanfeng):

其根在腳，發於腿，主宰於腰，行於手指

The internal power is rooted in the feet, generated through the legs, controlled by the waist, and manifested through the fingers.

But although the original masters obviously had a straightforward understanding of the situation, we latecomers are having a hard time following in their footprints, due to the lack of precise operating instructions. I have therefore clarified the process described in the quote above by dividing the key training elements into subsections that we can discuss more specifically. The three main elements of the ARC are *Accumulate* (at the lower trunk), *Rebound* (from the feet and legs) and *Catch* (in the arms and hands).

In summary:

- **ACCUMULATE** scattered upper body energy into the lower trunk.
- **REBOUND** a concentrated energy mass or flow from lower trunk down to feet and then upward again.
- **CATCH** the energy surge as it rises through your arms, into your hands, and shape it as you issue it for any purpose.

That is essentially what the Tai Chi Classic writings stipulate – yet few people take it seriously. When people read that line about '*energy originating at the feet and rising through the legs*' they usually take it as a metaphor or else as an awkward description of physical bracing or a lunging technique of some kind. Nothing could be further from the truth.

When people read the *Classics* line about 'energy issued from the fingers' they assume it's merely a polite way of talking about physically vigorous 'fajing' (發勁) – issuance of physical power in a spasmodically tense hand-waving gesture. That interpretation is also completely wrong.

The energy can be extremely powerful, more so than physical force, but its origin is gentle, slow and deep training. It emerges from the sensitive calibration of the following deep qualities:

Relaxation: The upper body relaxes, allowing you to **accumulate** and sink the scattered forces. (*Accumulate*)

Grounding: Awareness of the stability and penetrating roots of the soles of the feet attracts the energy further down, to the ground, and then re-launches it upward again through the entire body in a **rebound** effect. (*Rebound*)

Extension: Once the energy has rebounded up from the soles of your feet, the *mind* is used to project the power up and out through your hands, into any combative or healing target or just for the fun feeling when you **catch** it. (*Catch*)

ACCUMULATE: You allow the scattered random energy to settle in to the mid-section of the body. That includes not only the specific *dantian* point (Conception Vessel 6; a few finger-widths below the naval) but also the entire lower trunk, including everything at and below the waistline to the inguinal crease – hips, lower guts, pelvis, butt, and perineum. You should begin to think of this area as the engine of accumulation, or gas tank of the car. Other centers are more important for control, but for marshaling and concentrating the power, this is the essential reservoir area. This 'pelvic unit' together with your legs and feet forms a single functional component of internal energy basing and projection.

REBOUND: From that initial accumulation area, you use your mind to (gently) drop it down to the soles of your feet, with your legs as the conduit. You deliberately and specifically release the power downward to your feet and soles with your mind. In the Accumulate process, you experience 'filling from above' but now in the Rebound phase it becomes 'filling from below' as the energy naturally rises to the pelvic unit. In this Rebound process it's better to mentally work the soles of the feet as integral units rather than focusing narrowly on the commonly cited *yongquan* point (Kidney Meridian 1; frontwards along the center lines of the sole).

CATCH: Then from the lower trunk, it rises further in an even more directed, powerful, vibratory form through your upper body. A light branch of it goes through your head and brain and spreads from your forehead down your front, while the bulk of it comes straight through to your arms and out to your fingers to complete the Catch stage. You feel it come right out to your hands and fingers, as a little soft impact 'bang' experience, spreading warmth and vibratory power across the full inner surface of your hands. You're better off focusing on the broad surface of the hands and inner surfaces of the fingers as a unit, rather than trying to segregate out the *laogong* point (Pericardium 8; center of palm). There are other situations when specific points can be useful, and I'll cover some of those in later sections.

Once you've mastered an easy flow of the ARC internal power on mental command, many other disciplines can teach you to apply it, whether you're interested in martial arts, healing, or just the incredible experience of the process itself. I'm describing something fully tangible and accessible here. It's not philosophy (purely intellectual), but it's not a matter for Gold's Gym (purely physical) either. It's a process and although it's triggered and controlled by the mind, it is not imaginary.

THE AIKI ENIGMA

There is another conceptual input to the basic set of ARC drills, and a great aid in understanding the internal energy in any of its manifestations.

That is the profound martial arts mystery known as *aiki* (合気), the 'transparent' power underlying the supreme mastery of Sagawa Yukiyoshi (1902-1998). Sagawa was the greatest martial artist of the Golden Age of pre-modern martial arts, the classical period from about 1600 to about 1990. Of all the masters I've researched and read about, by all accounts Sagawa was supreme. He came closest to showing the attributes that most martial artists are chasing: an absolute, instantaneous and effortless resolution of any unarmed challenge. There have been amazing fighters, before, during, and after Sagawa's time. But nobody to my knowledge demonstrated this ability so purely and easily and yet talked about the source of his mastery in such oddball terms.

Why oddball? While many martial arts training methods are clothed in fuzzy, semi-or-pseudo spiritual terms, Sagawa's way of talking about his power was very plain and down to earth. He called the source of his ability *aiki*. But unlike many teachers of his era, he did not make references to gods, spirits, arcane texts, deep philosophies or exalted mental states and visions. Nor did he talk about elaborate internal maps of the body's organs and tissues, energy pathways or alchemical architecture. He basically said that *aiki* is conceptually simple but difficult in practice, and always insisted that *'aiki is a technique'*.

But clearly *aiki* is not a technique in the normal mechanical sense of judo or ju-jitsu. Though Sagawa's flagship system of Daito Ryu Aiki Ju-jutsu had a vast legacy inventory of such mechanics from their ancestral super-sensei Takeda Sokaku, Sagawa paradoxically stated with unshakable resolution that his *aiki* power had nothing to with those kinds of paint-by-numbers martial arts application methods. Rather, Sagawa regarded his *tanren* (鍛錬) solo practices as the supreme key to his *aiki* power. Yet to the superficial glance, his *tanren* training techniques look very much like ordinary martial arts drills, found in a variety of traditional systems as practiced by hundreds of thousands of people throughout the world. Sagawa practiced these *tanren* hard and heavy. But although many highly skilled *kendoka, judoka, aikidoka, karateka* and others do likewise, we don't see a lot of Sagawa-level masters out there.

So, if the source of *aiki* power isn't a catalog of grappling and takedown moves, nor an inventory of physical conditioning drills, could *aiki* be some kind of psychological interplay between attacker and defender? The skilled practitioner can perhaps engage another human being at an almost telepathic level of intimacy for any purpose, cooperative or antagonistic.

In Aikido, much is made of the concept of *aiki* as a cover term for a variety of these inter-personal skills - sensing, positioning, anticipating, feinting, leading, baiting, cooperative re-directing through coordinated dynamics, etc. I have been privileged to teach Tai Chi to many Aikido rank-holders (*yuudansha*) over the years. While they are wonderful people and powerful martial artists, I believe that most of them would agree that no matter how eagerly they have pursued the idea of *aiki* as a principle of interpersonal engagement (as per Aikido theory), they have not gotten much closer to understanding Sagawa's method and results.

The more you research Sagawa the more doubts you'll have about applying that common Aikido idea to such a rare bird. The psychological or *relational* interpretation of *aiki* is probably not the source of Sagawa's power. It's both too physical and too intellectual, while Sagawa's power seemed to disregard, or at least transcend, both mind and body.

I am still a work in progress in cultivating this power, and I very much respect those who are explicitly aligned with Sagawa's formal legacy or lineage and who demonstrate great combative work. But, whether right or wrong, few of them talk about it the way I do. So keep an open mind. I have found an interesting clue to the *aiki* power that may be helpful or at least interesting to anybody - regardless of training background or lineage.

I'm trying to bring whatever remaining brain cells I have, and whatever bit of experience I've gained, to bear on a question that interests us all, regardless of weight class or style. I want your focus to be on the *ideas* and *methods* - though I realize it's human nature to look at the messenger too. This book is my strongest statement on the fundamentals I've tried to put forth in all my books. These ideas may carry one of you readers a far greater distance than I'll ever cover myself. That's reward enough for an instructor and author.

This book does not break with the models and methods of my previous Tai Chi and Xingyi work. But it's a more explicit synthesis. If it looks like a duck, walks like a duck, and quacks like a duck, it *is* a duck, so I'm going to reveal what *aiki* is, what it has to be, and how to train it. I understand that this will ruffle some feathers, anger some people while just baffling or amusing others. But a few readers will stop and reflect on it quietly and deeply.

You need a certain key insight to begin training *aiki*, and that moment of actually feeling the truth of it in yourself is what I call the **aiki singularity**. Even though you will not become an overnight Sagawa-clone or UFC cage-beast, you will have crossed a threshold and your internal world will never be the same. Remember that Sagawa never stopped training, never called himself a finished product. For him every day was another step on the infinite road of power. But you need to understand what *aiki* is before you can set foot on the path.

First I want to clear away the issue of biomechanics and specifics of physical structure and motion. Is it possible the real *aiki* secret is some purely physical posture or motion? Let's look at Chinese internal arts. Every little village clan has their own secret, special, sacred legacy system. If you look across all these styles, there is no one set of perfectly correct physical principles, except at the very broadest generic level.

People want to hold out as the ideal a certain secret sauce of particular body alignment, or fascia integration routines, or whatever else can be claimed as the One Best And Only True Thing. But *all* the major systems have had great masters of internal boxing despite their divergent and often mutually contradictory specific principles and their wildly divergent particular practices.

One system has long stances, another short. One stands you high, one has you low. System X leans you forward, System Y does not. This one moves fast, this other moves slow. But they've all had *equivalently great* masters over the centuries. The mind and the internal power are *everything*, while the bio-mechanics and structures of any 'system' and its precious inventory of moves or particular practices mean little. Any drill, regardless of origin, that truly works the power will get you over.

With *grounding, relaxation, extension,* and *mind*, you can transform any system, or no system, into your personal power plant. Even if you got your start tightly welded to system X, Y or Z, you can ditch those conventions once you understand the continuous torrent of ARC power. The goal should be to have your power fully activated at every moment, in full integration with your every motion. *Every moment, every motion.*

We'll begin with the **Aiki Training Condition** as a fundamental pre-requisite. In a later section, I will explain the combination and culmination of all this work as the 'Aiki Singularity'.

THE AIKI TRAINING CONDITION

Let's pick up the first breadcrumb of the *aiki* enigma at the start of the trail, winding it all the way back to Tai Chi supermaster Yang Chengfu's training Dictum #7:

七: -上下相隨

Number 7: Coordinate upper and lower.

That captures the first key to *aiki*. We may roll our eyes and skim lightly over an old chestnut like that. But it's talking about something practical and specific. After I unpack it in a simple definition I'll discuss the training methods.

> **Aiki is the supra-physical power that arises from lower body segmentation.**

This is the significance and result of 'coordinating upper and lower'. In particular, it's an understanding that:

1. the energy arises specifically from the lower body.
2. it is not an ordinary physical or muscular power.

Now what about Sagawa? Is *aiki* a matter of leg muscle building, or, if you're a naturalist, becoming a 'functional strength' caveman or cross-training super-beast? No. It's absurd to assume that Sagawa's muscles or tendons or fascia tissues were so far superior to those of every tough guy he took on, especially in his 80s and 90s, when he was increasingly wheelchair bound, but as combatively invincible as ever. I do understand that his tough abs and strings of a thousand push-ups were widely admired, but there are plenty of ripped guys out there and only one Sagawa. It's not that anybody who can knock out dozens or hundreds of pushups on command is a master of *aiki* internal power.

Take look at a sample of Sagawa's comments on the special significance of the lower body as the power source:

足腰の重要さは何度もいっているでしょう。

I have continually emphasized the importance of the legs and hips.

そんな技なんかより基礎、とくに足腰を鍛えるのだ。

The most crucial thing in aiki is the foundation, most especially the legs and hips.

足腰のできていない人は肩の力に頼るようになってしまう。

Those who have not conditioned their legs and hips properly will rely on shoulder (muscle) power.

力というのも本質的に腰からの力でなければならない。上半身の力はすぐにかわせるが腰からくるものはかわしにくい。

Essentially, power must emanate from your hips. Power generated from your upper body is easily evaded. But the power coming from your hips is inescapable.

みんな腰が弱い。

Everybody's hips are weak.

結局、足と腰が大切のだ。
自然に腰に力がはいるような体にならなければいけない。

In summary, the important thing is your legs and hips (lower body). You have to naturally infuse your body's hips with power.

In these quotes, was he talking about athletic squats, dead-lifts, or fitness club leg machine workouts? If so, there should be millions of baby Sagawa supermasters running around all over the world, because everybody's doing those common conditioning drills.

> **The first key to *aiki* internal power conditioning is to become continuously and dynamically aware of your lower body, soles of feet to hips.**

I will call this lower body primacy the Aiki Training Condition (ATC).

Over time, a weird kind of unique power permeates your entire body, arising from the lower half. That permeation eventually leads to a key moment of integration that I will explain in another section as the Aiki Singularity. Aiki development requires that you forget about your upper body altogether for certain development purposes. Let it go.

Drop all upper body tension. It's easier said than done, because your upper body won't 'go away' so you can work on the ATC. It's still attached to you. And no matter what kind of training you are doing with the ATC, anything you do with one part of your body necessarily affects the whole. Furthermore, the later application and deployment of energy requires full-body flow, out to the hands. That is an explicit element of the ARC model. So we're left with the conundrum of how to build a specific, precise internal training program around the ATC.

All the drills in this book have been chosen and crafted to address these issues. The three drill families are each aligned to one element of the ARC. Each of them is built around the ATC – the requirement that internal power is explicitly sourced from the lower body. These three drill families (each is one leading idea with a cluster of related practices) are synthesized from three sources:

1. Elements of Sagawa's *tanren*.
2. Tai Chi principles.
3. Xingyiquan basics.

I have treated the Tai Chi and Xingyi details more deeply in my other books. Here I am extracting a few basic elements of these systems and hybridizing them to create an optimal training menu for activating internal power.

First, I want to define what I mean by 'lower body' and delineate its parts. The lower body is everything below the waistline, assuming the waistline runs approximately at the level of the naval. There are some important sub-elements. For example, when I talk about Accumulate, the main focus will be on the pelvic assembly. That includes the lower abdomen, hips/pelvis, waist, and butt – all as one conceptual sub-unit. It's basically what Wiki calls the 'pelvic skeleton' and all its inner organs:

The pelvic skeleton is formed posteriorly (in the area of the back), by the sacrum and the coccyx and laterally and anteriorly (forward and to the sides), by a pair of hip bones. Each hip bone consists of 3 sections, ilium, ischium, and pubis.

When I talk about Rebound, the main area of interest is the sole (bottoms) of both feet, and your legs, up to where they connect at the femoral sockets.

Remember, just because the ATC emphasizes the lower body, that does not mean the upper body energy is neglected. Far from it, as you will see (and feel). But the upper body's energy is a kind of overflow catchment zone for the lower body's source power.

THE ARC DRILLS

The three drills presented here are a super-efficient way to experience the core concepts and energy effects of the ARC process. They can be the foundation of your work on the Aiki Training Condition – the starting point for your personal internal *aiki tanren* (合気鍛錬) conditioning set.

They are organized by ARC segment, according to their main focus effect – Accumulate, Rebound and Catch. But each one of these drills strengthens the foundation for full-body permeation of the internal power. They are segment-focused as you work them but each of them affects the energy of the entire ARC.

They represent a synthesis of concepts and practices derived from Tai Chi, Xing Yi, and also Sagawa's primary *aiki tanren* drill. In the sections below, I present the conceptual background of each of the three core drills as well as the central practice and also a cluster of related extensions. These drills require minimal time, space, equipment or other overhead.

ACCUMULATE Core Drill: Relaxation

The first segment of the ARC is Accumulate. That means to give up the upper body strength, relax, and allow a kind of energy to settle in the lower trunk. In many systems, this work is attempted via forced breath regimens, with abdominal tension. But there is a more effective and natural way to accomplish it.

It is based on static standing, known as *zhanzhuang*. This is a popular internal method, in different flavors and guises. Each of the many physical stances used for *zhanzhuang* normally comes paired with a set of visualization or imagination protocols to engage and develop the internal energy. The method I'm presenting here is similarly structured, but extremely simple to operate.

We'll adopt the Three Substances pose (三體式 sāntǐshì) of Xingyiquan. Every tutorial on Xingyiquan begins with this pose.

Rear foot: bears 70% of weight; angled out slightly

Front foot: bears 30% of weight; angled inward slightly

Body: somewhat bladed

Front hand: Tiger Mouth shape; index finger aligned with nose

Rear hand: Tiger Mouth shape; curved inward below naval

The characteristic 'Tiger Mouth' hand shape is covered in my other books, especially *Radical Xingyi Energetics*, but for this drill you can mimic what you see in the illustration. These are the essential features:

- Soft, relaxed opening of hand, with extended (not tensed) fingers.
- Opened curve between thumb and extended index finger.
- Angled wrist.

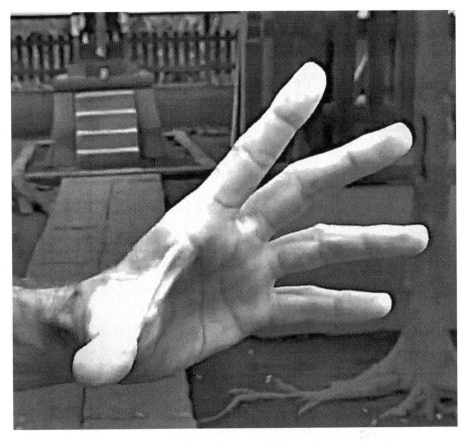

Figure 1: The Xingyi Tiger's Mouth hand: fingers extended but not tensed, a curve opened between thumb and index finger, wrist slightly angled.

It is used in the Santishi and also in the dynamic technique known as Splitting (劈拳 pīquán), one of the traditional Five Fists. For Santishi, you use it as a way of maintaining consciousness in your hands at all times, yet without excess tension. A number of the drills in this book specify this hand shape.

This simple stance can be used for a very powerful Accumulate effect. The *internal* protocol consists of the following elements:

- External form of San Ti Shi

Figure 2: Santishi externals: back-weighted, bladed, Tiger Mouth hands.

- Hips turn toward rear hand (mind/feeling only)
- Rear hand pushing forward (mind/feeling only)
- Relax arms and upper body

• Energy at hips becomes tangible

Let's review the external framework of the stance. We have to be careful here. Often this devolves into clock-watching to see how long one's legs can endure. That means nothing for internal development.

When you read other books and publications on the Santishi, it seems to involve a lot of complex alignment points and precision mechanics. There's a whole checklist of things you have to watch out for, as far as which bone is in line with which organ and so on. Most of that doesn't matter very much to get started. We want to focus on the energy. Teachers will crawl all over you with a slide rule and a tape-measure to ensure no little hair is out of place, but most of that doesn't matter.

Begin by opening the rear (right, to start) foot to 45 degrees, and the other leg extends straight out with its foot turned inward. If you drew your foot back, the heels would graze one another. It's ok if it's a little wider or narrower. Don't worry too much about that, because this is an internal training protocol. The front-to-back distance between feet is equal to about your own double-shoulder width. You could stand at a lower or higher level than shown in the illustration. None of that will matter much for the internal effect. This is not an endurance trial, nor leg development, nor any sort of ritual dance stance.

The front foot is turned somewhat inward, so the feet are placed as diagonal parallel lines. Your weight should be 70% on the rear leg, and 30% on the front. You don't have to get fussy about it, it's just a feeling that you're mainly supported by your rear foot. The front leg is not locked but not much bent (that would be a half horse stance). It's almost straight. You have a feeling that your front leg is rotating inward, in concert with the inward angled front toes. Your waist does not face straight to the front of the pose. Rather, your waist is canted or 'bladed' a little to the side. The most important thing for your upper body is to relax.

Your hands will be shaped as the Xingyi 'tiger mouth' that has been covered already. So your index finger is straight (not stiff) and you've opened a natural curve between the thumb and the finger. Your wrist is slightly bent, so there is an angle at your wrist. Your other fingers are straight. The front arm is extended out, straight but not locked, along the line of the front leg. Your nose is level with your index finger and you're looking straight along it like a gun sight, without tension. Your rear hand (in the same 'tiger mouth' shape) is relaxed and positioned at your lower *dantian* area, where the energy will accumulate after we add the Inner Activation.

Santishi Inner Activation

The important thing now is the internal activation effect. At this point, you should be asking what you do as you stand. Hope to run out the clock before your leg collapses? Or ponder your grocery list? No.

We'll begin with the lower trunk. Imagine you are turning your waist and hips, which includes the *dantian* and pelvis - everything from the inguinal crease up to your waistline, the entire unit of the lower abdomen, which I will call your hips (腰 yāo). You don't move physically, rather, you generate a *feeling* that you want to rotate your hips. Imagine that powerful hands are gently but firmly grasping your hips and those hands are trying to rotate you in the direction of your rear hand (to the "inside").

It's just a feeling. You aren't physically turning your hips. You need to play in your mind a little bit. Create the feeling that your hips are turning slightly or that you are about to rotate them. I'm sorry that it's so 'mental' but, after all, Xingyiquan is "Form-Mind Boxing". Don't change your upper body, try to maintain a good Santishi configuration in your upper trunk area, arms, and hands. Relax everything above your naval. But maintain that feeling of turning, a very slight activation of your hips.

Meanwhile, your rear hand is *resisting* the turning – but not physically, only energetically. You don't actually put your rear hand on your hips to stop that 'virtual' turning (as described above). Position your rear hand in back of your body's center line (vertically cutting down the naval). Don't place the rear hand directly *at* the naval line, and don't push the hand *forward* of it. You should be *behind* the midline so that as your hips begin the feeling of turning, your rear hand is (mentally) resisting and trying to (mentally) block that rotation. This is done without physical tension and strength. You aren't physically pushing or touching anything and yet you'll feel there's a mass there. That is the energetic mass of this Accumulate phase. You'll actually come to feel an energy mass as a quasi-physical thing in the space between your rear hand and the front of your pelvic or lower abdominal region.

There's a basic *ki* exercise, known to almost everybody, where you face your palms a few inches apart and you start to feel a slight pressure between them. That's a real effect in ordinary Qi Gong, but it won't take you very far. This Santishi accumulate exercise generates a somewhat similar feeling but much more intense because the mass here is much stronger.

You - mentally only - *feel that you're turning the waist into the rear hand, while the rear hand is very gently resisting.* At that line of resistance you create a kind of energetic interlock, as though both sides are squeezing a ball between them, but without muscular activation or tension. This is not the *sanchin* karate kata. Don't think of it that way or you won't get anywhere. Do it with your mind alone and that's when you'll actually feel the mass.

Figure 3: The area between the turning waist and the resisting hand generates an energy mass.

Relax and only apply the pressure mentally, coming from the hips and waist, toward the hand, and meeting the (virtual) pressure from the hand in the other direction. You've thereby built a kind of interlock feeling, as the two energies seem to create a new structure from their mutual opposition.

Relax and keep everything else the same in your Santishi pose. Keep your front arm extended. Don't let it droop just because you're paying attention to the hip interlock. Relax the front leg as much as you can. Try to disengage any strength from the rest of your body. Keep your mind on the waist turning, very gently and the rear hand's gentle resistance. Even though your hand and waist are not touching, and although there's a gap between them, inside that space you'll feel a mass. Feel that you are compressing that area. It will become as real as if you were compressing a small basketball. The longer and more continuously you can do this without losing that 'lock' feeling, the more powerful an energy result you'll get. Do that for a few minutes, or even just one minute, then switch to the other side.

The rear hand is engaged as though pushing but without strength, without motion, otherwise you'd just push right through, and get no benefit. It's a feeling of pushing, 'as though' there's something real there. It will become real, so that you're softly pushing a mass of energy, in a state of clear and yet fully solid tangibility, centered on the place of engagement between the energy coming from the *dantian* vs. the energy coming from the hand. They are pressing together. That mass will slowly expand to fill the entire body.

At first you may feel the energy emerging in jolts, when you catch that moment of the rear-turning waist and the front-pushing hand pressing against each other, like the meeting of two tidal fronts in a rip current. Later you can generate a smooth emergence from that interface and keep it perking. Still later it becomes a 'state' so your entire body is completely 'turned on' with this extremely powerful energy. This is the inner activation of Santishi taught to me by my Xingyi teacher. This is what makes the Santishi a cultivation process, rather than a 'stance'.

Important Point on the Hips

Now, here's another innermost point to this inner activation, a key within the key, embedded like Russian dolls. Once you have the basic idea of the Santishi external framework, and after you've got some feel for the inner activation protocol, you need to refine the (feeling of) the hips' turning action.

I talked about two large hands trying to turn your hips inward. To refine this and get even more power out of it, narrow the place of engagement in the virtual turn. Imagine you are turning from *the very lowest two points* on either side of your hips, right where the femoral junction comes in. This isn't quite the inguinal crease per se. It's a bit more to the side, and also 'inside' toward the bone itself. It feels like the lowest

Figure 4: Two streams of hydraulic energy meet to create a rip current energetic structure between them.

side area of the hips. As though a finger on your left and right sides is trying to rotate your entire hip assembly, but by means of two small control points – the lowest side extension of your hips at the femoral juncture. This seems like a trivial detail, but working from those two lowest points (keeping other aspects of the protocol as written above), will greatly magnify the power experience.

I could take the lazy way and identify these points with the familiar concept of kuà (胯). That is variously defined as *crotch, groin,* or *hip,* and found in standard phrases such as: 胯骨 (hip bone kuàgǔ) and 腰胯 (hips waist yāokuà). In a martial arts context, you commonly see *'inguinal crease'* as the best approximation, the line where the leg joins the pelvic assembly. Technically this is the *acetabulum.* I'm not a big fan of anatomy, physiology and material structure for internal training, so when I do need to spotlight one particular area you can be assured that it's important.

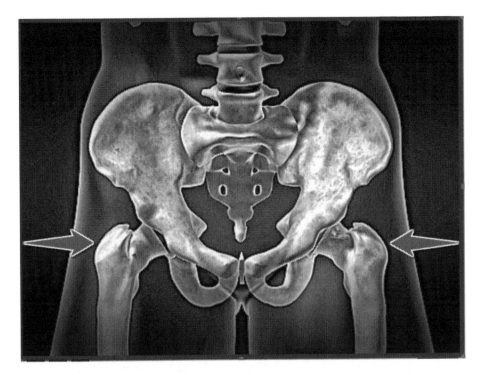

Figure 5: When doing the hip rotation part of the Inner Activation, imagine the lowest edges of the hips as the control points where you are "being turned".

However, while those technical terms, translations and interpretations aren't wrong, they don't convey my point here. In practice, concern with the inguinal crease tends to become another positional or structural hang-up. For example, the lower you sit in traditional stances, the sharper the physical angle appears (between body and leg), bending at the inguinal crease. That looks great in performance, it works the leg muscles fiendishly, it gives you the look and feel of a tough kung fu workout – what's not to love?

It's all good, but that emphasis leads away from my point. My emphasis is strictly on what you do with your mind. For this, 'depth of sit' is not highly relevant. And even the famous Tai Chi adage 'relax the kua' (鬆胯 sōngkuà) doesn't capture the simplicity of my point. After all, although relaxation is important at all times, very few people when sitting in a beautiful, deep, low stance can really feel whether or not their *kua* (however they conceive it) is truly relaxed. That teaching has its place as an internal training foundation, but that's not my point here.

The point is simpler, conceptually more straightforward and physically a lot easier than any of that stuff. Maybe its very simplicity and ease makes it hard to understand (we love physical complication). Regardless of stance, or depth of sit, independent of exactly what muscles are engaged where, and what's connected to which, *you simply place your mind onto those two 'control points'* (the femoral juncture area at bottom/sides of hips) while doing the Santishi inner activation. This *mental technique* will massively amplify your energetic experience.

The pelvic bone, the assembly as a whole, feels as though it's lighting up like a neon sign. After the first few times, it will begin to retain a persistent charge. The entire pelvic bone acts like an auto battery or charge plate or maybe an antenna. It's not that I'm getting physical all of a sudden, you'll realize that the pelvic bone is co-located with a parallel energetic unit. The energetic shadow counterpart of the physical bone, co-located with it, is lighting up. Every cell in the bone is vibrating with something that feels like neon or radioactive power. Though my Xingyiquan teacher told me this, and wrote about it, I hadn't understood. When it finally happened, I was taken by surprise.

It's a very different experience from the early stages of normal ki and breath (cosmic orbit) training. This may be why Sagawa denied that his *aiki* was "ki" (気in the sense of 'life energy' or 生命エネルギー). Sagawa always emphasized that his *aiki* was not ki (気) and yet not any form of ordinary physical power either.

I believe that was partly because his sober warrior mind may have been offended by the playful exuberance of the flamboyant ki-power demonstrations of Nishino Kozo, who was receiving widespread media attention in the 1980's and early 1990's, around the time Sagawa made those statements. That's understandable, because most ordinary Qi Gong programs don't develop anything like what Sagawa had. But Sagawa himself stated that:

私の考えでは気というのは自分の体にためておいて必要な瞬間にだすものだ。

To me, ki is something stored up in your body that you project instantaneously when necessary.

In any case, he continually stressed that *aiki* power is something deriving from the "legs and hips". This bone light-up effect is the beginning of that. It's as though there were a very large battery or capacitor that does not function until it's been charged for a long time, and then suddenly the threshold charge is attained and it kicks to life. Thereafter it can continue charging, going further all the time.

Every time the energy ripples, streams, or suffuses your body, it leaves a residual trace. Maybe it's like annealing or metal plating, a process of tempering layer by layer. A 'charge' is building up, and that charge accumulates most obviously and thickly in the biggest bone, the pelvis. At some point it gets so powerful that its altered state reaches conscious awareness. That's a watershed moment, an interesting milestone on the endless spiral of working this internal stuff.

To wrap your head around this, consider the following lines from Guo Yunshen, quoted by Sun Lutang:

凝神於此久之 *The power accumulates in the energy body over a long period,*

元氣日充 *Every day of training further charges your original qi.*

元神日旺 *Every day of training is strengthening your original spirit power.*

神旺則氣暢 *Strong spirit power triggers a smooth flow of energy*

氣暢則血融 *A smooth flow of energy triggers suffusion of blood*

血融則骨強 *A suffusion of blood creates strong bones*

骨強則髓滿 *Strong bones absorb energy deep into their marrow*

髓滿則腹盈 *Energy absorption into the marrow overflows into the abdomen*

腹盈則下實 *Filling the abdomen leads to strong root*

下實則行步輕 *Strong root triggers light footwork.*

Though it sounds very physiological, it precisely describes the feel of the process, including the abdomen packing that happens later. The pelvis is the first bone to undergo this 'lightup' thing, possibly because (in terms of the above analysis) it has the most marrow of any bone in the body, or maybe due to its structural position in the body, or maybe it's something completely mysterious that causes this. In any case, it lights up as described previously and completely transforms your practice experience and the quality of your daily life.

The Forward Arm Flow

At a more advanced stage, you will begin to feel how to 'hollow out' the armpit and shoulder of the forward arm, creating an energy vacuum which attracts the pelvic mass upward, from where it seems to roll outward through the forward arm to your extended hand. This will occur naturally as your energy mass becomes stronger and wider. You just need to stay relaxed and have a slight consciousness of 'emptiness' in the area of the upper ribs, the forward armpit, and the area beneath your upper arm. That attracts the forward/upward motion of the power mass.

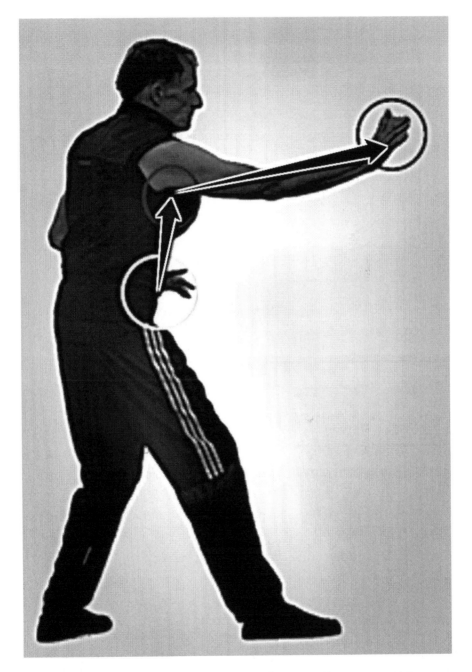

Figure 6: The forward underarm area relaxes and empties, thus attracting the energy mass upward (and outward)

Hip Check

You can use a very simple Tai Chi mini-drill to determine how much energy you've infused into your hips. The Constant Bear (長熊 cháng-xióng) drill was created by Professor Zheng for students who lacked the time, space, or basic physical stamina to do the entire form. But it has the side benefit that we can use it as a calibration tool for internal energy permeation.

It embodies all five of the core Tai Chi principles that apply throughout the full form:

- Relax
- Body Upright
- Straight Soft Hands
- Separate Weight
- Turn Waist

Constant Bear is when you do all those things simultaneously in-place without stepping anywhere. There are two basic modes to choose from: front-loading and rear-loading. When front-loading, you turn into the weighting foot with initial emphasis on the front part of the foot. When back-loading, you kind of back up into the weighting foot, with weight initially distributed more toward your heel. As you shift weight going side to side, you are rotating your waist gently. The weight differential between legs at the end of each rotation can be anything from 70/30 to 100/0. The arms follow your waist, they don't pick up any athletic momentum or inertia of their own.

For energetic diagnostic purposes, the interesting thing is the potential to feel *the crackling*. It sounds like a Stephen King title, but it's my name for an intense energetic sensation whereby one or more joints gets so packed up with energy that it feels inside like an intense electric arc, spitting sparks and shooting tendrils of power out in all directions.

As you rotate, keep your mind at the inguinal/femoral area, the lower edge of the hips already introduced. At some point you will feel, and almost hear, a kind of crackling along the imaginary line that runs across the lower hips, from one side's inguinal area to the other. It isn't quite actually audible but it feels as though it should be. It's as though somebody is frying an egg inside your tissue, or maybe grilling or barbecuing your meat in there. I'm not saying that like it's a bad thing. It feels incredible. That's the energy crackling, surging, boiling up in there. If you don't feel anything like this yet, it just means you aren't yet experienced enough with the Accumulate drill.

Later you'll be able to play with this effect in other joints, such as shoulder, elbow, and wrist when statically holding any of the seven sample Tai Chi poses covered in *Tai Chi Peng Root Power Rising*.

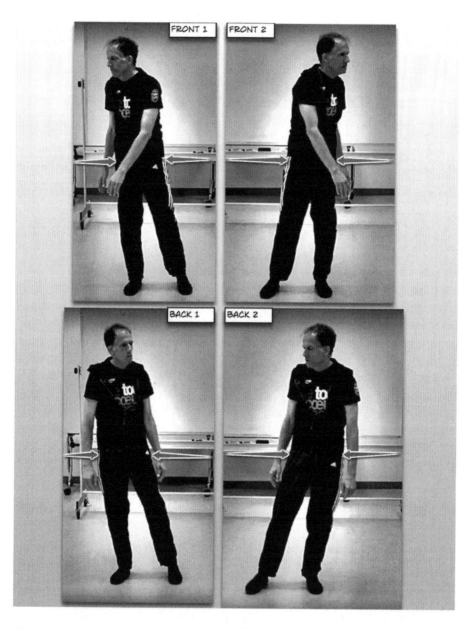

Figure 7: Constant Bear - Rotate waist with your mind at the indicated lower hip edges while shifting weight side to side.

REBOUND Core Drill: Grounding

Focus on fire rising through your form
Upward from your feet
Until the body burns to ashes
But you remain.

- Vijñāna Bhairava Tantra

Now you'll learn a deep internal principle of Xingyiquan and Taijiquan via a simple exercise from a different martial art. You'll come to understand that the internal power transcends any codified 'style' whatsoever. We're looking for the most effective way to practice the Tai Chi wisdom on differentiating substantial vs. insubstantial. It's been specified in the Tai Chi Classic writings:

虛實宜分清楚

Insubstantial and substantial should be clearly differentiated.

This is such a Tai Chi truism that I hardly need to spill any more ink on it. It's also something I've approached in my other books from various angles and with a plethora of Tai Chi drills. Now I'm giving my most profound insight on this and the most straightforward and accessible training framework for it.

The most obvious interpretation of the above idea of differentiation is found in Tai Chi legwork. So the REBOUND drill will incorporate elements of that. The legs give us an immediate and obvious example for practical understanding of differentiation: *one leg bears more of your body weight than the other.* Every Tai Chi style, and almost every other internal training system, has this concept baked into every movement and stance. But is there more to say?

In fact, there are multiple dimensions (not only the legs), that could theoretically sustain a substantial/insubstantial differentiation. Here's a partial list:

- One leg *vs.* the other
- Right half of the body *vs.* left half
- Upper body *vs.* lower body
- One arm *vs.* the other
- Back of body *vs.* front of body

The list above doesn't exhaust the full/empty binary oppositions you could think up, based on any given Tai Chi pose. For example, you could think of an 'attacking' hand as full, while a 'defending' hand is empty. Or you could imagine more detailed divisions, such as one plane (e.g. back or front) of a given limb being inherently (or positionally) *yang* or *yin*, while the opposite plane takes on the counterpart quality. All these distinctions have their proponents. But what we're interested in here is: *which of these distinctions is going to best facilitate our direct work with the tangible internal power?*

The *upper body vs. lower body* distinction is the key exemplar and power engine referred to in the Yang Chengfu injunction to clearly differentiate empty and full. That in turn was the basis of my earlier formulation of the Aiki Training Condition (ATC) as expressed by Sagawa. This primacy of the upper/lower dimension was again made explicit by Yang Chengfu when he taught:

陰陽分上下虛實須

Yin and yang are divided into upper and lower, which necessarily creates insubstantiality and substantiality

So there's the theoretical justification, from the Tai Chi angle, for my radical statement of the Aiki Training Condition. You'll eventually understand and experience your lower body packed with a very solid-feeling thick vibrating power (*yang*) which rises to permeate the upper body in a different form - clearer, crisper and lighter (*yin*). The lower and upper energies can then be combined at your hands in the moment of issuance. But the most important thing to work on is the lower body foundation – that's where most of us fall short. Working on the lower body's foundational energy requires that you eliminate upper body tension, to enable eventual full permeation.

But how is this worked, down on the ground where the tires meet the pavement? We can begin with an approachable distinction that anybody can feel instantly for themselves. That's an entry on the list above: *one leg vs. the other.*

We begin with a simple physical practice that will lead us to the energetic understanding of the leg differentiation – going from physical, which everybody already loves and understands well, to something essentially non-physical. Once you've begun to work with the ATC by using the differentiation of substantial and insubstantial in the two legs, where it's so accessible, we move on to the upper vs. lower distinction, which leads in turn to full body permeation.

These levels of energy experience are accessible through any good Tai Chi form and particularly via the Zheng Manqing (ZMQ37) simplified Yang Tai Chi form. But the full Tai Chi form, with its many postures and exotic movements and gestures, creates distractions that entangle most people in the weeds far from the energetic uplands. They remain enmeshed in Tai Chi as cultural artifact, theatrical performance system, mild calisthenic regimen, social opportunity, mystical fantasy, combative self-deception.

Therefore, while Tai Chi is the highest practice, it's also the most likely to throw you off the scent of the energy itself (which has more potential to create all the legendary Tai Chi benefits than any calisthenic or dance/theatrics). Most Tai Chi students have heard all these philosophical ideas as background doctrine, but after years or decades of practice have little personal experience with the astonishing results of truly working it.

For these reasons, we can work initially via a different route, using a simple drill framework that isolates and magnifies the desired result. This drill will enable you to concentrate on the essence of the ATC (which is also the foundation of Tai Chi and all the internal arts), after which you can import that understanding into a full Tai Chi regimen and finally turn the ignition key for the first time.

Please don't take the drill's simplicity as a license to shut down your attention and assume '*I already know that*', or '*I've been doing that for years*', '*My teacher already mentioned that*', etc. Don't blithely assimilate this to something you think you already know. Please follow the conceptual points and the specific directions fully and exactly as written until you get precisely the effects described. Then you can do whatever you want with it.

To make sure you understand the universal nature of the concepts, let's do another pre-flight via a different glide path. I want you to see that the drill embodies the principles of not only the ATC and Tai Chi, but of Xingyi as well. All those methods have one goal.

We begin by looking at the simplest level of substantial vs. insubstantial differentiation, which is the legs. I presented Xingyiquan's Santishi stance above as a "single-weighted" practice. That means your weight is not evenly shared between the legs. It's little known, but classical Xingyiquan training incorporates *both* uneven (single) and even (double) weighting. It's essential to understand both conditions thoroughly. The Xingyiquan classic writings state:

有三體式。單重。雙重之別。

The Santishi of Xingyiquan is practiced as both a single-weighted stance and a double-weighted stance.

I only mention this so that you'll be open to the incorporation of a "double weighted" stage of the training later in this section. But we'll begin with the familiar concept of 'single weighting'. This is the simplest way to work with distinguishing substantial and insubstantial. But even here there are subtleties and misunderstandings.

單重之姿式。前虛後實。重心在於後足。前足亦可虛。亦可實。

In single-weighting, the front foot is insubstantial by comparison to the rear foot. The body weight is centered on the rear foot, but the front foot can be either full or empty.

A raised foot is obviously the simplest case of single-weighting, but here they're making the deeper point that the lighter foot can be worked in two distinct modes:

單重者。非一足着地。一足懸起。不過前足可虛可實。
着重在於後足耳。

Single-weighted does not mean that one foot is touching the ground and the other foot is suspended in the air, but that your front foot can be empty or full while the greater weight is on your back foot.

We can understand from this that there are several refined states usually glossed over with the simple-minded 'single weighted' concept. There are *degrees* of 'single weighting' and these degrees can be sensed and leveraged for incredible energetic gains. But now let's focus on one main thing: in practical terms what does it mean for an 'insubstantial' front foot to be either 'empty or full', while the main body weight is always on the rear foot?

Let's take the case of the foot touching the floor, putting aside for now the more obvious case of the entirely raised foot. How can there be two distinct modes of substantiality in that foot? The old masters were pointing to a usually ignored factor, that the 'insubstantial' foot can be either physically engaged (sufficient to keep it either off the floor or barely in contact with the floor) or entirely relaxed. In neither condition is the given foot and leg being used to support the body's main weight, which remains on the rear leg.

These two different modes of insubstantiality correspond to two stages of Tai Chi's **Cat Step Protocol**. That is, either:

1. the foot is barely touching the floor (in which case at least some small degree of muscular engagement must be present), or else

2. every muscle in the insubstantial leg and foot is relaxed into complete mush or tofu.

In the latter case, the floor supports the weight of the leg itself - but in neither case is any body weight taken on (body weight remains in the rear). Furthermore, the two distinct stages have a mutually transformative relation. First, the obvious assessment: the physically engaged state, which is a kind of 'substantiality' in its own local area (just the leg itself), contrasts with the 'total tofu' mode, which is a local 'insubstantiality'. But when you've practiced this awhile, you realize the opposite is also true. The engaged state of the leg is actually devoid of the true internal power (thus 'insubstantial') because it is tensed, while the fully relaxed 'tofu' leg experiences a massive torrent of internal energy, thus a kind of 'substantiality'. Don't worry if the above seems too abstract or philosophical. I'll give the precise working specifics for the entire drill sequence below. But you should understand that the principles of it fully embody what the great masters have written.

I said that there is also a *double-weighted* version of Santishi. Double-weighting has its own powerful energetic function once you know what you're doing. This claim too is evident in the classical Xingyi writings, as below:

練武藝者。是雙重之姿式。重心在於兩腿之間。

For training combative power, there is the double-weighted posture. The weight is centered directly between your feet.

The passage goes on to describe the *center-weighted* Xingyi training method as a high-tension procedure, which is the *external* use of the double-weighted (centered) pose. But my Xingyiquan teacher also showed me the *internal* method and effects of using the centered stance. And because that can be easily adapted into a simpler practice framework, it is included in the instructions below. The key concepts of this Rebound drill have been part of either Xingyiquan and/or Taijiquan all along. There's a whole world of refinement in the simple 'leg vs. leg' differentiation that can be exploited in Tai Chi and Xingyi training. The effects can be easily experienced and understood via the minimal Rebound drill here, and then injected into your fuller practice of the various arts.

I call this drill the *Cat Step Shiko* because it introduces a Tai Chi nuance which ignites the simple physical framework of Sagawa Yukiyoshi's supreme solo internal conditioning drill, a modified version of a basic sumo calisthenic. Sagawa emphasized, to a few of his students, what he apparently considered the crown jewel of his suite of personal *aiki* conditioning drills. It's named *shiko*, as it somewhat resembles the well-known Japanese sumo exercise of alternating leg-raising and squatting.

But if you do only Sagawa's modified *shiko* without integrating the Cat Step Protocol, I wish you good luck. You can work it until the cows come home and you won't get anywhere.

The mechanics of the drill are shown in the illustration, and they could hardly be simpler. The internal component of it is the Cat Step Protocol, borrowed over from Tai Chi. The Cat Step Protocol is normally

相撲の四股では、足を高く上げた際のバランス感覚も重視されるが、佐川式ではあくまで足踏みに重きが置かれているようだ

今回、佐川伝「四股」を演じていただいた佐久間氏は佐川宗範より直接四股の指導を受けている。姿勢を崩さず、膝を伸ばすことなく、足を踏みしめるように体重を落とす

四股

Figure 8: An article in a Japanese martial arts magazine contrasted traditional sumo shiko with Sagawa's primary internal conditioning method of the same name.

practiced (if at all) in only a very few hyper-conscientious styles of Tai Chi. Tai Chi is a more complex overall regimen than the simple shiko drill. The Cat Step Shiko offers the internal power of the Cat Step Protocol, embedded within the simple, easily learned, and spatially compact shiko framework.

I'm introducing the Cat Step Shiko as the supreme 'Rebound' drill but it intensifies all segments of the energy ARC. If you take this seriously and follow all directions carefully, you will experience and master five main internal effects:

Crack Step Surge: *Outgoing* pulsation of internal power from hip to foot.

Cat Step Surge: *Backwash* current of power from foot to hip.

Center Surge: *Upswell* 'light up' moment, from both feet to upper body.

Cat's Paw Surge: *Backwash* 'light up' moment, from hands to shoulders.

Daling Throttle Grip: *Continuous* calibrated power torrent through arms.

If, after learning this drill and working it for a while, you don't experience these phenomena, then either I haven't explained it well enough or you haven't executed it precisely enough. It has two main versions: the basic version A, and an extended version B. Beyond these, there are many supplemental practices once you've got the basics under control

Cat Step Shiko (A) – Work Stages

Begin with your feet about shoulder-width apart, your upper body, including arms and hands, completely relaxed and natural by your side.

Lift: Raise your foot anywhere from 1 cm. to 1 meter above floor. Engage the femoral/hip joint area to power the rise, thus trying to keep most of your extended leg and foot as relaxed and loose as possible. As you rise, and at the end of the rise, use your mind to create a feeling of *extension without tension*, as though your soft and relaxed foot is a calligraphy brush attempting to softly write something (but no need to play writing games with your foot, it's just a feeling of mild extension).

Touch: Now lower your raised foot to where the entire sole touches fully and flatly on the floor – but as contact only. It's as though strictly the bottommost layer of molecules in the sole of your shoe is allowed to come into contact with the floor surface. No weight whatsoever of any kind is supported by the floor. This step is easy to elide or slide over too quickly. Pause for a beat to fully experience this subtle state of touching without any imposition of weight at all.

Relax: Keeping your foot's position unchanged from the previous stage, entirely relax all muscles in the leg. The foot, ankle, calf, knee area, thigh – all turn to absolute tofu. You had to engage at least some minimal musculature to achieve the pure contact mode of Stage 2 Touch but now you are letting all that go. That means that while your main body weight is still very heavily resting on the support leg, the weight of the stepping leg (and only the leg itself) is now supported by the floor – because you are no longer using any muscles to hold it in the contact mode of Stage 2.

Center: After a beat or two, you leisurely begin to shift your weight across from the former support leg to the leg that was just raised and lowered. As you begin this shift, keep your mind on the soles of both feet and the area from the soles to just below your knees. I call this area of the leg *greaves*. Place your attention there. As you near the absolute center point, where your weight must become perfectly centered 50-50, use your mind to sense that exact midpoint. You don't need to stop there for now (Version A) but go slow and see whether you can mentally sense that moment of perfect equilibrium. You might not be sensitive enough at first, but the effort is training your mind. As you cross that midpoint, you'll be putting more and more weight gradually onto the opposite leg. As you begin to load that opposite leg, moving away from the midpoint now, again place your mind onto the soles of both feet. So on both ends of the shift, moving weight away from one foot and then again moving weight onto the other, (the 'intro' and 'outro' areas of the crossover) your mind is focused simply on the soles of your feet and the greaves. But just *at* the midpoint, shift your attention to sense the exact moment of double-weighting. As you move through the midpoint, return your attention to the soles and greaves again.

Re-Load: At the end of the shift, your weight is now entirely on the opposite leg and you begin the next rep with Lift (Stage 1) of the former support leg.

There are three distinct energetic experiences to be had from this drill. There's an outgoing flow in the stepping leg (Stage 1), then an upward inrush on the same leg (Stage 3), and a massive central surge of power from both legs up through your entire body as you cross over for the next rep. Let's go through them in the order you're likely to first experience them as you begin to work with the Cat Step Shiko (A) drill.

Cat Step Shiko (A) – Energetic Experience

1. Up-SURGE on Work Stage 3 (stepping leg) – The most obvious and most easily accessible energetic effect of this drill is the 'Cat Step Surge'. That is a massive torrent of non-physical or quasi-physical power flow that you'll feel every time you thoroughly release all muscular tension from the stepping leg and foot. At first it may not be super strong, and you'll have an uncertain feeling of questioning 'Is something happening or not...' If you have that feeling it means you are right on the verge of getting it. Sagawa said:

とにかく合気は一種の内部感覚で自得しなければならない。

Most importantly, aiki begins with a sensation that you perceive inside yourself.

You now have a framework for beginning that process. This surge feels as though it begins at the sole of your relaxed foot and quickly ripples *upward* through your relaxed leg to the hip joint / inguinal crease.

2. Down-SURGE on Work Stage 1 (of the stepping leg) – When you've really begun to experience the Cat Step Surge, that fundamental process, you can turn your attention to the Lift stage. In that stage, you now begin to feel an *outward* or *downward* flow of internal energy from the hip joint / inguinal crease to the raised foot, energized like a very soft low kick. I call this the Crack Step Surge, because it's an outward directed

dynamic from a solid 'handle' (upper thigh of the rising leg) to a soft 'whip' end – the relaxed lower leg and foot.

3. <u>Center-SURGE on Work Stage 4</u> (of lower body) – As you approach and fully sense the weighting midpoint, the 50-50 shared weight on both feet, you'll eventually feel a huge secondary surge, from the soles of *both* feet this time, lighting up your legs and the entire pelvis, hip, and lower abdominal area. For this A version, just feel it happen as you slowly traverse the weighting mid-point.

Cat Step Shiko (B) – Preliminaries

The B version identically subsumes the A version, but there's an added element, occurring at that crucial midpoint of weighting. Hopefully by doing the A version, you've become sensitive to the exact moment of crossover when your weight is momentarily directly centered, shared 50-50, on both feet. At that moment, the B version has you pause and work your arms and hands. This spreads the power through your body by extending it to the longest and farthest extremities of your arms and hands.

Before I lay out the B protocol, let's review elements of my prior books, which introduce some key ideas without getting into the deepest internal rationales. It's hard enough to get people to take even simple *relaxation* seriously, not to mention this relatively 'far out' stuff. But now enough people are working with the ARC that it's worthwhile going all the way with it.

Readers of *Juice: Radical Taiji Energetics* and *Tai Chi Peng Root Power Rising* may remember that one of the few energy hotspots that I explicitly called out as essential is at the center of the inner wrist just below the line demarcating the start of the hand. This is the acupoint called *daling* (大陵 dàlíng Pericardium 7). It has a special internal 'throttle' control function that I'll explain more fully in the following sections. When you see the references to the *daling* in the instructions below, refer to the description here.

Figure 9: The *daling* energy spot lies at the center of the inner wrist, adjacent to the line where the hand begins.

Though I presented it in a Tai Chi context, I learned it from my Xingyi teacher. It took me a long time, through studying his writings and my own work, to grasp exactly what was going on with that, and why he stressed it. I mentioned this point in Juice, and I explained further details in *Tai Chi Peng: Root Power Rising*, but I have not given the full activation protocol until now. That's because, on the few occasions I brought this up to private students, I could tell they had no feel for what I was describing, no frame of reference, and little interest. Now I will lay it out and see who among this wider readership wants to work with it.

The second preliminary for Cat Step Shiko Version B is the Xingyi hand shape. Please refer to the previous section (the Accumulate/Santishi drill) for details. There's an additional function of this hand shape that is normally overlooked, but which was explained by my Xingyi teacher verbally and in his writings. That is the angled wrist configuration, which we will exploit to the max in the handwork of Cat Step Shiko, Version B.

The angled Xingyi wrist serves a training-wheels function, giving you initial control over the full arm and hand power flow. For beginners it's even more effective than Zheng Tai Chi's Fair Lady's Hand, which seems like a polar opposite but is just a more advanced way of playing with the same arm and hand flow. This section teaches you how to work with the *daling* point explicitly, through the angled wrist configuration, for maximal and very surprising control effects. I will discuss the use of the Fair Lady's Hand for this purpose further below. For now, just take note of the softly angled wrist used in the Xingyi version of the Quiet Standing drill.

Note the opened *daling* point on many of the East Asian temple guardian figures. This is revealing (or concealing?) the internal training secret which I'm laying out here. Most people focus on the palm when viewing these sculptures, but the key is the *daling* point of the inner wrist.

The wrist bend is an effective method for focusing your mind until you can control the effect without overt physical gestures. Furthermore, in the learning stages the *daling* point functions as a choke control that enables a grip-throttle effect. This is part of the Cat Step Shiko Version B and its extensions.

Figure 10: The Xingyi hand shape and wrist angling are used to direct the mind through the *daling* points for a throttle-like control effect.

Figure 11: Guardian statutes frequently embody the configuration used to ignite the *daling* throttle control point.

Cat Step Shiko (B) - Method

Begin with your feet about shoulder width separated, your upper body completely relaxed and your arms and hands natural by your side.

Lift: (same as A)

Touch: (same as A)

Relax: (same as A)

Center: (same as A)

Shape Hands: This is the difference between the A and B versions. You pause at the midpoint that you've learned to precisely sense and calibrate through your work on version A. As you pause there, you will feel the Center Surge. Now you can learn to extend that power through your upper body and arms. This requires the following sub-steps at this paused midpoint moment. You should move deliberately, not super slow but without haste. Move at a natural pace and feel the amazing results.

Forward: Beginning from the completely natural, unshaped, hands-at-sides position, move your arms only, without any change in hand shape, forward of your thighs very slightly, 5 degrees or so.

Rotate: Rotate your arms, without changing natural hand shape, so that backs of hands face forward.

Extend: Now lightly and softly extend your fingers - 'seeking straight-ness' but not locked or stiff.

Curve: Rotate your hands inward, creating an angle at the wrist, extend fingers softly, and open the index finger with respect to the thumb, creating the 'tiger's mouth' shape.

Lock: Without changing positions of hands or body, 'feel' that your hands are softly connected to your feet. You can use the 'tiger mouth' shape as a convenient aid to imagination, as though you are softly squeezing your own feet from above and sides.

Fists: Having 'felt' the energy outline of your foot, now gently and softly curl your fingers into fists. At the end your fists should appear well shaped as though you could use them to hit, but inside they're soft.

Release and Relax: Gently open your hands. There is a process to this. Begin the relaxation by gently releasing the shape of your fists back to natural hand shape – but, most crucially, imagine that you're relaxing back to the *daling* point (center of inner wrist, just before the bottom line of the palm). Basically it means you put your mind to the *daling* point, your foundation, as you softly and completely release and relax your fists. They weren't tightly clenched, only fist-shaped, but still, some small degree of engagement was required. You now slowly release that engagement, putting your mind at the *daling* point. This creates a momentary but extremely powerful micro-surge of power localized in your hands (forward from *daling* point), filling them with warm, thick energy (you'll be amazed the first time you feel it). After filling the hands, it quickly surges up (backward from *daling* point) to your shoulders. This is the arm equivalent of the Cat Step Surge, with essentially the same properties. When you experience this, you'll understand that all these Core drills affect every part of the ARC, and your entire body. Following the Cat's Paw Surge, there is retention of a residual layer of power in your hands and arms that slowly accumulates, over many reps, during many days of practice. Later, the momentary Cat's Paw Surge effect can be maintained *continuously*, as explained below.

Re-Load: (continue as in A version; you naturally and softly release all shaping of the arms and hands from previous step, as you load all body weight to the 'new' side and re-fix your mind on the 'new' stepping leg and foot).

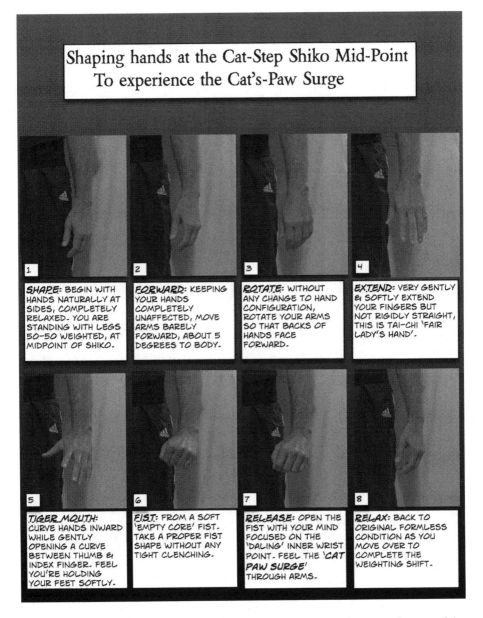

Shaping hands at the Cat-Step Shiko Mid-Point To experience the Cat's-Paw Surge

1 SHAPE: BEGIN WITH HANDS NATURALLY AT SIDES, COMPLETELY RELAXED. YOU ARE STANDING WITH LEGS 50–50 WEIGHTED, AT MIDPOINT OF SHIKO.

2 FORWARD: KEEPING YOUR HANDS COMPLETELY UNAFFECTED, MOVE ARMS BARELY FORWARD, ABOUT 5 DEGREES TO BODY.

3 ROTATE: WITHOUT ANY CHANGE TO HAND CONFIGURATION, ROTATE YOUR ARMS SO THAT BACKS OF HANDS FACE FORWARD.

4 EXTEND: VERY GENTLY & SOFTLY EXTEND YOUR FINGERS BUT NOT RIGIDLY STRAIGHT, THIS IS TAI-CHI 'FAIR LADY'S HAND'.

5 TIGER MOUTH: CURVE HANDS INWARD WHILE GENTLY OPENING A CURVE BETWEEN THUMB & INDEX FINGER. FEEL YOU'RE HOLDING YOUR FEET SOFTLY.

6 FIST: FROM A SOFT 'EMPTY CORE' FIST. TAKE A PROPER FIST SHAPE WITHOUT ANY TIGHT CLENCHING.

7 RELEASE: OPEN THE FIST WITH YOUR MIND FOCUSED ON THE 'DALING' INNER WRIST POINT. FEEL THE 'CAT PAW SURGE' THROUGH ARMS.

8 RELAX: BACK TO ORIGINAL FORMLESS CONDITION AS YOU MOVE OVER TO COMPLETE THE WEIGHTING SHIFT.

Figure 12: Steps in the Shaping process at the midpoint (even-weighted) stage of the Cat Step Shiko Version B. One hand is shown for detail, but all actions are performed identically and simultaneously with both hands.

Cat Step Shiko (B) – Energetics

The added energetic phenomenon here, in addition to massive intensification of the **Crack Step Surge**, the **Cat Step Surge**, and the **Center Surge**, is the **Cat's Paw Surge**.

I apologize for these hokey names, but I want to convey that these are distinct, tangible and productive experiences – they are the purpose of this drill. It isn't your dad's senior center Tai Chi - shift weight back and forth, try to 'sink' a little... this is more like precision engineering. I'm holding your feet to the fire until you really grok what I'm putting out here.

In Version B, the energetic experiences are similar to Version A, except that now when you perform Stage 5 'Shape' you will experience something really amazing. From the first motion ('Forward') you'll feel a huge 'light up' of your feet that instantly reaches and fills your arms. Then with the 'Rotate' and 'Extend' gestures, the power will pack into your forearms, hands and fingers. As it fills your hands, your feet remain energetically linked so that every twitch of a finger, in fact every *thought* of a finger, triggers a corresponding throbbing response in the foot energy.

The most blowout phenomenon will come once you've formed the soft fists. In the beginning, when you're still getting the hang of this drill, as you gently release the fists back to naturally opened hands, place your attention on the *daling* point of each hand. At some moment you'll realize that the simultaneous physical and mental actions there have 'pushed a button' in your energy body. Initially, the reaction will be a full-arm surge from fingers to shoulders. This is basically the arm version of the Cat Step Surge from foot soles to hip. This arm surge will have a full-body permeation, as a kind of echo effect through your trunk and back to your legs, much like the Cat Step Surge. When your extremities are energetically linked in this way, the entire body is suffused with the internal power. This is the true 'Macro-Cosmic Orbit' sometimes mentioned in connection with Taoist alchemy.

The Daling Throttle Grip

Please pay attention now, because if anything has ever qualified as an internal training secret, this is it.

As you get more control over the Cat's Paw Surge effect, you'll realize that you can work it more deeply by *maintaining* the soft fist shape, for as long as you want, with merely the *idea or intention of releasing* it into the *daling* point. You don't actually open the soft fist. Then the 'surge' will become a *continuous current through your arms*.

It's a radically interesting and powerful effect. It's as though the *daling* (when set into motion via this entire *shiko* protocol) is a power button or switch that only needs to be continuously 'held down' (activated by your mind) to allow the current to flow unimpeded. You can maintain a continuous massive current for minutes or longer. And when you do release it at last, you'll again experience the powerful full body echo effect (similar to the leg surge).

The effect is strangely like operating the handgrip throttle on a motorcycle. On the right side of the handlebars you have the twist throttle. To use the twist throttle, you twist the handlebar backward and the engine revs up (or you accelerate).

Apart from the difference that the energy effect is identical in both hands, it's otherwise exactly analogous in every way. The grip position is virtually identical. You directly control and calibrate the degree and strength of energy flow by using your mind to very slightly manipulate the degree of closure and the angling of the fist. It all happens within a very narrow scope of external motion (if any) – maybe 1 or 2 degrees of physical change as your mind works the hands back and forth, with closed and then opened intent. You can also very slightly 'close' and 're-open' your soft fists in place (visually there's very little difference between the tighter and more open soft fists), and/or you can very slightly change the angle of wrist bend. These back-and-forth changes are micro-movements, hardly visible to an external observer.

The energetic effect, the torrent through your hands, wrist, forearms, and arms up to shoulders will really blow you away, especially as at some point you realize that the *lower body* is actually supplying all the power. This power is not inherent to your hands. It's called up and out from the lower body by your mind. The real 'engine' is below (just as the power source when throttling up a mounted motorcycle is centered in the lower half of the body). The engine is the lower body. This is the fulfillment of the Aiki Training Condition.

Figure 13: The Xingyi hand position in the Cat Step Shiko Version B engages the *daling* point to function as a kind of throttle grip, like a motorcycle.

Just as with motorcycles, there are varieties of energy quality, from rough periodic jolting, to soft occasional ripples, through to the higher stages of even more powerful, but smoother, pure purring whole-body effects – like a super high-end bike. At the highest engagement, all motion ceases and you are left in single solid-state, centered finally on the *niwan* (brain center point). You can learn to instantly activate, continuously maintain, and precisely calibrate all of this via your mental manipulation at the *daling throttle* (which I'll call DLT for convenience from now on).

It's probably easiest to first experience the DLT by means of the soft Xingyi fist configuration (positions 6 and 7 in the chart). Once you've got the hang of it, however, you are in no way limited to that position only. The modes of engaging the DLT's continuous power effect are listed below, in ascending order of subtlety, difficulty and ultimate power:

1. Soft fist throttle (Cat Step Shiko B)
2. Xingyi open hands (Xingyi Quiet Standing)
3. Xingyi Santishi (Xingyi angled wrists)
4. Tai Chi Fair Lady's Hands (Tai Chi Quiet Standing)
5. Xingyi Five Fists (moving with "always on" throttle)
6. ZMQ37 Tai Chi full form

Levels 4 and 6 in the above list use the Tai Chi straight-wrist, extended fingers 'Fair Lady's Hand' shape (see cell 4 in the Shaping Hands graphic above).

In the beginning, the more of the basic A mode you do, and the more clearly you feel the double-weight transition position and the Center Surge, the more powerfully the B mode will eventually blast you. Although I'm talking about hand work in this section, the power source is always the lower body. As you get more advanced, you won't even need the preparatory Cat Step Shiko any more. At the start of a session, you can just settle into the Xingyi or Tai Chi Quiet Standing pose, engage the *daling* in both wrists, and light up the current for a 10-minute or more unbroken stream experience.

It will seem to emanate hugely from both inner wrist points (*daling*) and permeate your entire body. At some point you'll realize that that wrist points are "calling it up" from your feet and lower body directly through the *niwan* (brain center point) and down into your hands. Try to keep the current constant and gradually strengthening. There will be occasional soft ripples (or even hard wave jolts) but those won't affect the overall strength or duration of the engagement. This is not imagination. You'll know when you've got it as it's quite a surprising sensation. Count how long you can maintain it before dropping back to ordinary physical standing (which looks identical).

Count in your mind: 1...2...3...4...5... how many the seconds you can maintain the unbroken current, until you can easily maintain it for at least one minute, then time it for ten minutes and longer. This can be done with your hands in either of the angled wrist positions (either cell 5 or 6 in the chart) or (using mind alone without the 'throttle' wrist angle) in the Tai Chi position (cell 4). It's like having a motorcycle in neutral gear and then using the throttle grip to rev it up super high and just holding the engine in that state.

Advanced students of Xingyi will recognize that the *daling* engagement is also the key to intensifying the *mingjing* (明劲 clear electric jolt energy) in Splitting (劈拳 pīquán), the first of the traditional Five Fists, which involves a sudden, crisp opening of exactly this same *daling* point in both hands simultaneously. You'll feel that more intensely also.

In every Qi Gong system, you hear a lot about the hands. You'll experience mild sensations of heat, pressure, buzzing and tingling from any calm and focused arm and handwork. The key differences in terms of this current discussion are:

1. *Relaxation emphasis: Most teachers pay lip service to relaxation but the students rarely get near the real thing.*

2. _Lower body sourcing:_ Conventional focus is on arm stretching and twisting, thus putting cart before horse.

3. _Daling point:_ Most systems are primarily concerned with the láogōng point (勞宮), in the centers of the palms. It's very unlikely you'll ever reach the 'continuous throttle' state without mastering the daling ignition. Once you've mastered that, every point in the body, every zone, each component, and every single cell will be charged like lightning.

Forearm Pressure Mode

When you're in the position of either panel 5 or 6 (Cat Step Shiko Version B chart), you can use your mind to generate a feeling of pressing your forearms, along the ulna's edge, down and slightly outward into the floor. Don't change your posture or add any tension or strength whatsoever. But mentally create a feeling of pressing your forearms strongly into the ground, as though they were bearing your entire body weight, like a forearm plank hold, or the yoga pose _pincha mayurasana_. This will generate massive internal power packing within your arms and hands.

Backtivation

When you are doing this mental/gentle pressing, you can mentally sluice the power from your hands down your back. This contradicts the usual dictum about power circulating in an upward flow from lower back to upper, but it does no harm and in fact strengthens your overall control. Go ahead and gently roll the power _backwards_ from your 'pressed down' arms, down through your entire back (not just spine, the entire inner surface of your back will ripple with internal power sluicing). I call this _backtivation_. From there, mentally extend the same downward surge through the backs of your thighs, calves and down into your heels. Remember it is not muscular tension of any kind, it is mental activation of the internal power flow in a deliberately reversed direction. Here is where you can begin to understand that this version of internal power is a radically divergent advancement over the conventional, pedestrian concept of *qi* energy, which is usually held to be monotonically normative in its patterning. Free your mind.

Experience the soft but massive pulses in your heels and soles at the bottom of this inverted back-sided ARC. Work this way for a minute or so every now and then, it's very instructive. When you have a good command of that, work on alternating between the upward and downward ripple, across the entire surface of your back, the back of your hips, and the backs of your legs and heels, then all the way up again to just below your shoulders, through arms, and continue. You can command downflow and upflow, alternating in turn.

Figure 14: Generate a feeling of intense (but non-physical) pressure as though bearing weight on your forearms, pressing downward and outward on the floor.

The Short Wave

Here's something really interesting to play with. You can create an extremely short and 'local' *standing energy wave* inside your soft fists. Use the shoulder-width, equal-weighted standing position that's the basis of Cat Step Shiko Version B. Your hands should be shaped into the soft fist as in panel 6 of the chart. Normally when you think about unclenching your fist (heading toward panel 7) you would generate a whole-body energy resonance beginning from the *daling* point. That will rock you from head to toes. Then you can create a localized concentration zone within the fists themselves with its own unique standing (continuous) wave.

It's a matter of sensitizing your mind. Go through all the steps of the Cat Step Shiko Version B a few times. When you're ready to generate the standing fist wave, first place your mind at the *daling* points (both inner wrists) as usual. From there, lightly and quickly 'flash' your mind forward to the outer surface of your knuckles. That's the area of your outer knuckles that would impact a target if you punched. The lower boundary of this ride-along wave is the line at the base of the wrist. The outer boundary is the outside surface of your knuckles. You will then feel the power conform and confine itself to the small area of your closed hand. Not that anything is taken away from the rest of your body. It's a stepped-up energy effect, like a powerful harmonic riding on the whole-body fundamental frequency. You use your mind to maintain, further compress, and amplify this. Again as with the other DLT type of effects, this can be held for time. Check how long you're able to sustain the 'standing wave' churn in your fists.

Figure 15: A compressed 'local' standing wave can be generated in the restricted area of your softly closed fist (base of palm to outer knuckle surface).

Higher Foot Raise

Once you have control of all the energetic effects, you can experiment with extending and raising your foot higher in Stage 1. Be careful with this. Go gradually in that direction. In general, the further and higher you raise and extend, the more powerful the energetic effects will become – but *not* if you find yourself even slightly sacrificing the basic qualities of relaxation and precise discernment of the required stages. If you aren't careful, athletic raises will devolve this drill back into a trivial physical calisthenic.

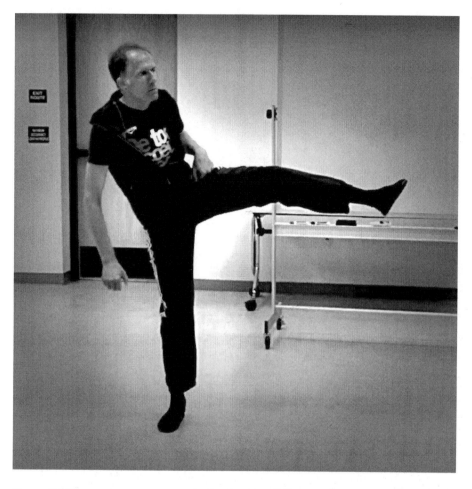

Figure 16: For greater power surge in the Cat Step Shiko, gently raise your leg to waist height with soft extension - but strictly maintain all other principles of the drill.

Angled Leg Extension

Instead of, or in addition to, the side rise of the basic shiko, you can experiment with a more frontward-directed kick. Sagawa used a karate-like front heel kick for this, but beginners will get more mileage from adopting the Tai Chi 'Separate Foot' kick, which is lower and less strenuous.

Figure 17: Sagawa's version of 'Raise Foot' is a great extension, but it's best to minimize tension in foot, leg, and upper body by substituting a Tai Chi kick.

Your foot will gently extend at a 45-degree angle, to about your own knee height, while your thigh is almost at waist level. Try to power the move with your upper femoral thigh area alone, while relaxing the rest of the kicking leg and foot as much as possible.

Figure 18: The Tai Chi foot raise 'Separate Foot' can be used as a frontward-angled, soft and relaxed kick that integrates well with the Cat Step Shiko. Arms may be relaxed at sides as in the basic Cat Step Shiko.

Friction Step Shiko

Yi Quan (意拳) is a 20th century adaptation of classical Xingyiquan, derived from ideas passed down in the same lineage as my traditional Xingyiquan. One classical theme that Yiquan picked up on nicely is the 'friction step' found in some forms of Baguazhang and other internal arts. The Yi Quan version is extremely simple. You merely raise one foot and, slowly and gently, circle it forward, sideways, backward and finally forward again on the inside.

The idea is to keep the bottom surface of your shoe just barely grazing the floor, so that it would almost create some scraping or friction if you applied any pressure. This can obviously be the basis of yet another *shiko* adaptation where one or more such circles take the place of a single leg lift (shiko Stage 1) on one side. After your circle(s) you would replace the foot with the additional stages of the Cat Step Protocol (contact, relax), feel the Cat Step Surge, then load and continue with the other leg. Alternate back and forth. This is a very powerful lower body energy cultivation practice.

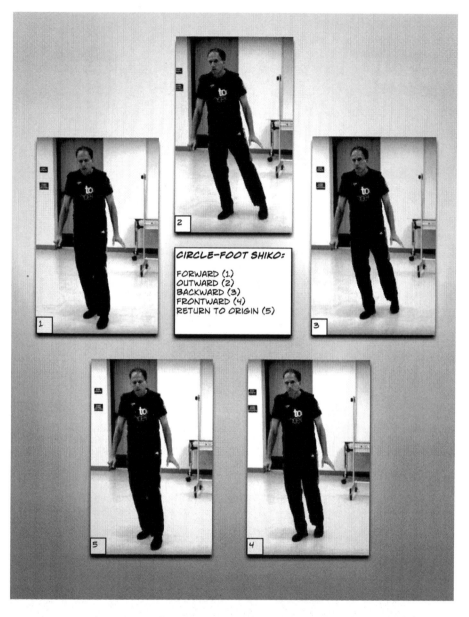

Figure 19: The Yi Quan 'friction step' can be adapted for the Cat Step Shiko.

Tai Chi

Once you have experienced and learned to control and intensify all the energetic effects of the Cat Step Shiko (A and B versions), then if you know Zheng Manqing Tai Chi (the form or a subsection) you can replicate those phenomena within the form. It's difficult at first because there's a lot more going on. The great virtue of the *shiko* practice framework is its simplicity, which allows you to focus on controlling the energy. But it's worth the effort to step up to the big leagues, as embodied in the full form.

The Cat Step Protocol (all stages of version A) applies to every transition from one pose to another throughout the Tai Chi form. That means that every time you change the position, angle, or weighting (PAW) of a foot, you have an opportunity to go through the Stages: raise, contact, relax and load. You'll eventually feel both the Crack Surge and the Cat Step Surge in every transition.

Beyond that, you also can learn to generate the Center Surge within the form, as it too can occur every time you move between any two poses, whenever you must cross over a double-weighted moment. Become conscious of that moment and you'll soon be experiencing the Center Surge within the form - where it's far more outrageously intense.

Also, the Cat's Paw Current (arm flow from version B, which is really a whole-body current sourced from the soles of your feet) can be experienced continuously within the ZMQ37 form practice. You can work the *daling* throttle effect (DLT) and other energetics using Tai Chi in the following ways that do *not* require knowledge of the entire form:

- Quiet Standing
- Raise Hands
- Step Turn

- Repulse Monkey

For most of the Tai Chi work, you need to understand the Fair Lady's Hand shape. I mentioned it above (panel 4 of the Cat Step Shiko Version B chart) but I'll cover it here in further detail. The Tai Chi hand shape differs externally from Xingyi but the internal work will be essentially identical. In ZMQ Tai Chi, you hold your wrist straight and flat, your fingers lightly aligned and straightened without stiffening. It's easy to get it by pressing your forearm lightly to a wall.

Figure 20: Learning the Fair Lady's Hand by conforming forearm to a wall.

Having worked sufficiently with the Cat Step Shiko (Versions A and B), and having ignited the *daling* energy hotspot (calling up the lower body energy to the arms and hand), you'll find that in Tai Chi mode, using the Fair Lady's Hand, the power streams in a torrent through your forearms, on an inner center line through the *daling* point and straight out into your middle finger. In fact it's spreading through your entire palm and hand, but it's like a flame that burns hottest in the center while extending laterally. This is one variation on the Catch phenomenon of the ARC process.

Quiet Standing

The simplest and easiest thing you can do with Tai Chi is the Tai Chi version of quiet standing – but with the DLT fully engaged every minute you stand. No more dead-zoned or spaced-out standing. This in itself is a crazily powerful experience. Sometimes you'll feel the energy is about to lift you straight off the ground.

In Quiet Standing once you really have the ARC running, you can diagnose its strength and further fortify it with a simple gesture. *Very slightly elevate your toes.* Only your toes alone - not the rest of your foot which remains relaxed and flat on the floor. Your stance does not change in any other way. This minuscule, soft, barely perceptible toes-lifting will launch a huge momentary engagement wave that will reverberate through your entire body and arms. I call this toe-lifting full body engagement the L/ARC protocol, because you amplify the running ARC by slightly lifting your toes, like the bottom line of the letter L.

Figure 21: Tai Chi Quiet Standing can be a framework for igniting and maintain the DLT effect with Fair Lady's Hand and maintaining it for a time.

Raise Hands

Now let's look at the first move in the ZMQ37 Tai Chi forms. Although ZMQ Tai Chi generally requires the straight, flat wrist shape of Fair Lady's Hand, the opening moves flex the wrist. The reason should be obvious –that hugely ignites the whole-body flow via the Daling Throttle effect. Most people who do this opening move are not feeling that. But, having begun to master the currents and surges of the Cat Step Shiko and the DLT, you are positioned to experience the massive energy boost this gives.

Standing straight and relaxed with your feet shoulder-width apart, you basically raise and then lower your hands in parallel, together. But in the ZMQ37 form, this is done in a precise way, with minute attention to five distinct changes of hand/wrist configuration along the way. You must keep your upper body, arms and hands as relaxed as possible.

1. Beginning from the Tai Chi Quiet Standing position, imagine that strings tied to the back of your wrists and attached to the ceiling are raising your arms to shoulder height. This will naturally cause a slight downward droop or down-brushing of your hands and fingers. This is wrist change #1.

2. Now imagine that small chunks of weight hang from each elbow. The weights pull down your elbows, drawing your hands straight back, but the air resistance (or imaginary water) supports your fingers as you retract, thus opening up the wrist angle slightly. This is wrist change #2.

3. Your arms come in as close to your body as possible without tensing up, without tightly drawing them in unnaturally. They should come fairly close to your shoulders. When they have reached the end of the movement, simply relax your wrists completely, with no other change. This causes a re-closure of the wrist angle, in

preparation for the big opening of the next move. This is wrist change #3.

4. Now you lower your arms, straight down. As you begin, imagine that there is a bar or other impediment that your fingers must brush up against, lifting them on the way down. This is the big *daling* opening and if you have remained gently conscious of the *daling* through the previous moves, the energy triggered here, centered in the *daling* but actually pervading your entire body, and sourced from your feet, will practically knock you over. This opening is wrist change #4.

5. As your arms reach their lowest extension, your fingers also must lower all the way down. Try to keep the energy state or flow unbroken even as the angle begins to flatten again. That will greatly increase the energy harvest experience. This is wrist change #5, returning you to the starting configuration.

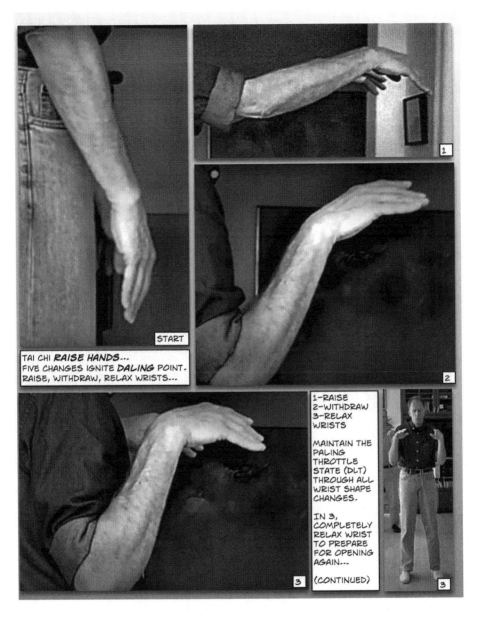

START

TAI CHI *RAISE HANDS...*
FIVE CHANGES IGNITE *DALING* POINT.
RAISE, WITHDRAW, RELAX WRISTS...

1—RAISE
2—WITHDRAW
3—RELAX
WRISTS

MAINTAIN THE PALING THROTTLE STATE (DLT) THROUGH ALL WRIST SHAPE CHANGES.

IN 3, COMPLETELY RELAX WRIST TO PREPARE FOR OPENING AGAIN...

(CONTINUED)

Figure 22: The first three wrist changes...

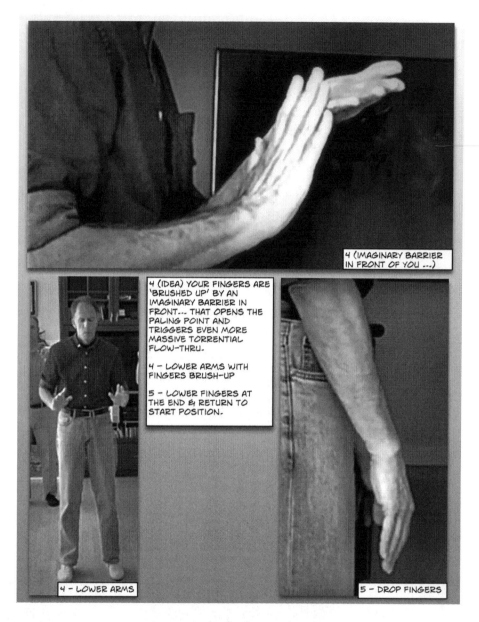

Figure 23: The final wrist changes.

Stepping Turn

Another interesting mini-subset of the ZMQ Tai Chi form is the spin-ning turn (the first movement of the 2-part technique 轉身擺蓮 zhuǎn-shēnbǎilián). The full form of this move may be challenging for some people. It requires you to spin a full circle on the ball of your right foot. You begin with the left arm and leg both extended straight sideways (panel 1) and then quickly spin a full circle while keeping both softly extended. At the end you shift weight to the left foot and bring the arms straight forward at shoulder height.

It's a good move, but if you can accept a dumbed-down, baby version you can harvest a more intense internal training effect than the stan-dard move provides. In the modified version, rather than a quick 'spin turn' this becomes a more deliberate and leisurely 'step turn'. In every other way it's about the same.

You still pivot entirely on the ball of the right foot (or left if you switch sides) throughout the spin. The difference in the mechanics is merely that your left foot *steps* several times, circling around the right leg to accomplish the full turn. Your weight shifts softly back and forth from right foot to left foot as the stepping requires. The arms, crucially, are held straight out (straight but not stiff, shown in final panel 7) through-out the stepping turn. They do not change position at all from begin-ning to end.

It will feel odd the first few times. The internal secret here is to main-tain full consciousness of your and hips throughout the move. You don't let your arms "die" in your awareness, as you must maintain the softly extended shape. But apart from that, you mainly focus on your hips while making this gentle and leisurely turn. Imagine that two large and powerful hands are firmly (but not roughly) holding your sides and rotating you. Of course, it's actually your feet doing the work, but imagine that your arms and feet have no involvement at all. It's all being done by a soft external force that grips your torso. Later you can step-turn for several complete revolutions, feeling the gain in energy intensity with each mini-step.

At first it's mechanically weird. Over time you'll begin to feel a very interesting energetic movement in the trunk, both during the move and also when Quiet Standing immediately afterwards. In fact, you may feel it more strongly in the immediate post-drill quiet standing than while doing the drill itself, at least for an initial period. The trunk and waist energy you'll begin to experience from this is not easy to access from other kinds of practice. It is traditionally called 'Old Ox Power' (老牛勁 lǎoniújìng).

Warning: don't turn so fast that you become dizzy. If you have any tendency to lose your balance for any reason, practice on carpet, away from any hard furniture, walls, or other dangerous surfaces. The point of this is *not* to become dizzy. If you become dizzy you are doing it wrong. Take the steps very slowly, evenly, and calmly. I know you'll want to associate this with whirling dervishes and other exotic or extreme practices, but this is something different. It's Tai Chi and we are doing it for the internal power gain alone. You could perhaps relate this to a very restricted form of Bagua circle walking, but your softly extended arms lack the tension, exertion, and theatrical elements that can afflict Bagua practice.

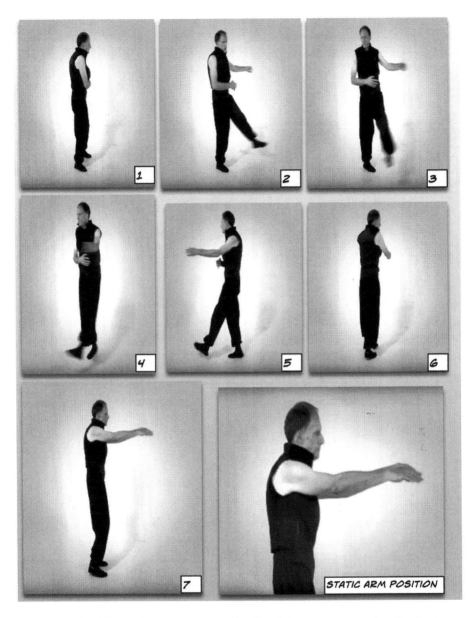

Figure 24: The full Tai Chi 'spinning turn' (1-7) and the starting position for the 'stepping turn' modification.

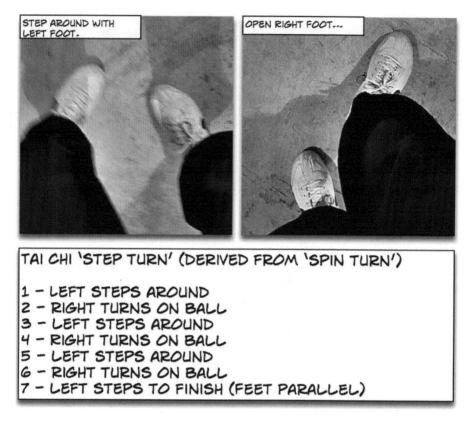

Figure 25: It should require about seven movements to complete a full stepping turn.

Repulse Monkey

Professor Zheng Manqing stated that the only solo practice he ever witnessed his own teacher doing consisted of the Single Whip static pose and the Repulse Monkey mini-sequence. That's a big clue to the power of this sub-sequence. Repulse Monkey gives you a framework to incorporate everything covered so far: the Cat Step, the Center Surge, the DLT, and the acetabulum control points in the hips.

It is back-weighted at all times. The weight is 100% on the back foot both at the start and at the end of each single-hand forward 'push'. To begin from the static Repulse Monkey pose, extend the rear hand 45 degrees back, toward the rear corner. But don't fully turn your head to look at your rear hand, just turn slightly so that your rear hand is barely in your peripheral vision.

Then, fold the rear hand toward your ear while rotating the other palm upward and stepping back. Your stepping foot touches toe first, no weight. Now you are ready for the main move. But notice that the back step gives you a chance to work the Cat Step Surge. It begins from a rise (Stage 1, like any step), then there's a touch of the toe – no weight at first only contact (Stage 2). Then, just before beginning the main 'push' gesture, relax your rear leg entirely (Stage 3). The floor bears the weight of the leg itself, but your body weight is all still on the original (other) foot. Even though the step is backward, which may feel different or awkward compared to the Cat Step Shiko, it's the same process at work and you'll feel the Cat Step Surge through your stepping leg.

In the next motion, several things will happen:

- You will gently load full body weight onto the stepped leg (Stage 4).
- Your hips turn as the mechanical basis for the arm gesture.

- Your rear hand presses softly forward.
- Your front hand gently sinks along your side.

Be careful to align the rear foot straight, so that it ends up parallel to the other foot, not angled outward as in other Tai Chi styles. The two feet point straight forward as though you are standing on parallel train rails. That helps keep your waist facing forward at the end of the move, and it's a good mental discipline for relaxation and body awareness.

Your hips must turn 'from the acetabulum' that is, the lower/side points already discussed. This is crucial. An external observer cannot tell the difference because it isn't a physical distinction. You must put your mind on those points as you turn your hips into the arm gesture. This will cause a huge bursting of power in the legs, hips, and lower abdomen during the turn. Repulse Monkey intensely fulfills the promise of the classical training stanza quoted in an earlier section:

髓滿則腹盈 *Energy absorption into the marrow overflows into the abdomen*

By working the hips and hands properly, your abdomen will be packed with power.

Repulse Monkey is like extending a long pointer or telescope with your hand, then bracing one end of the fully extended unit on the floor, and finally squashing it all back together in one smooth move. In terms of Rebound, it's like a big slam dribble move, raising the ball high and then spiking it down on the floor. As you begin the final movement, your front leg should rest on the floor with no tension whatsoever. The energy "ball" begins from your soft inner wrist (as you start into the final 'push' move), is then taken up by your hip rotating with the move as the main power source, and then drives like a spike through the home stretch of your extended, completely relaxed leg. As you come to the final instant of completion, focus your mind on the sole (the bottom) of your relaxed, extended leg. The power will shoot through that forward leg like a lightning bolt, and will buzz along the underside (sole) of your foot right to and through your middle toe. At the finish, that entire side of your body will be buzzing and feeling lit up like a Christmas tree. It's an extremely interesting energy phenomenon. Each repetition of Repulse Monkey is a fresh opportunity to play with this advanced energetic control technique.

Finally, although in the reach-back gesture your hand is flat-wristed as always in ZMQ Tai Chi, as it moves toward your ear in preparation for the main gesture, the wrist flexes slightly. Repulse Monkey is like the first movement of the form – an exception to the Fair Lady's Hand shape that otherwise pervades the practice. It is a deliberate exception, just as precision engineered as the five wrist changes in the opening move of the form.

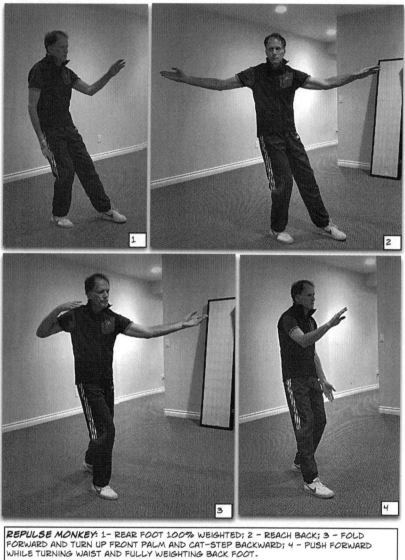

REPULSE MONKEY: 1– REAR FOOT 100% WEIGHTED; 2 – REACH BACK; 3 – FOLD FORWARD AND TURN UP FRONT PALM AND CAT–STEP BACKWARD; 4 – PUSH FORWARD WHILE TURNING WAIST AND FULLY WEIGHTING BACK FOOT.

Figure 26: Repulse Monkey mini-sequence: monkey strike with left hand, followed by monkey strike with right hand.

Figure 27: Master Zheng demonstrating Repulse Monkey.

Figure 28: The diagonal line would be the normal straight wrist of Fair Lady's Hand. the flat line is the actual flexed wrist angle that is correct for Repulse Monkey.

Some people have wondered about the slight wrist bend in Professor Zheng's performance of this gesture. Wasn't it supposed to be Fair Lady's Hand, with straight wrist, at all times? Is that just a free-form thing, like writing grass style calligraphy, or is it a key element of the basic move?

It is a key element. As you straighten the wrist while you push forward into the final gesture, you again have the opportunity to coordinate the *daling* ignition with the hip movement for another super-charged energetic moment. As you open the wrist of the 'striking' hand while pushing forward, imagine that you are pressing the *daling* point into a mass of soft cotton that touches your inner wrist. Go slowly, power the move physically through the lower hips – it's as though your arms are just passengers on the hips, riding on their motion as the conveyance vehicle. As you slightly straighten out the wrist flexion, you're gently igniting the *daling* point and you'll feel the whole body surge. This effect can also be practiced in the Tai Chi pose Brush Knee and Twist Step.

If you are skeptical about the Professor's hand shaping, ask yourself whether it's likely that the master who was the first to learn this hidden insight (Fair Lady's Hand was a training secret passed from his teacher Yang Chengfu), and who made it a core part of his own signature Tai Chi construction, would suddenly turn sloppy or inattentive in demonstrating a key move? This is as deliberate, purposeful, and energetically functional as the opening wrist changes illustrated earlier. It does not in any way invalidate the overall emphasis on the Fair Lady's Hand shape. The two configurations are jointly optimized for energy development in the form.

Figure 29: Deliberate soft wrist flexion, closing to enable the opening.

The AIKI Singularity

Singularity definitions:

1. The state of being singular, distinct, peculiar, uncommon or unusual

2. A point where all parallel lines meet

3. A point where a measured variable reaches unmeasurable or infinite value

4. (mathematics) The value or range of values of a function for which a derivative does not exist

5. (physics) A point or region in spacetime in which gravitational forces cause matter to have an infinite density; associated with Black Holes

> **The Aiki Singularity is the moment when, with a mental touch on the *daling* points, you experience, can maintain, and can intensify the torrent of power sourced from the lower body flooding upward to engulf your arms, hands and the *daling* points themselves.**

How daring of me to state that, right? After all, as I've said, I'm no UFC cage beast, so how dare I (or anybody) presume to claim such things? But think again - is it so presumptuous? A dedicated pursuit of this trail may be a way of honoring Sagawa sensei as the supreme martial artist he was.

But it doesn't matter, because you are free to accept or dismiss anything as you wish. If it's mistaken you can move on to something better. Consider yourself lucky to have heard these ideas, and maybe someday they'll bear unexpected fruit for you. If nothing else it's interesting detective work, following the breadcrumb trail of *aiki* and cross-correlating the logic of that with reality wherever possible.

You should be willing to consider anything. And just because Sagawa had a sudden *aiki* breakthrough at age 17, don't assume that the more gradual methods here must be mistaken. Sagawa stated that developing *aiki* is a process requiring conditioning over time:

私は１７歳で合気がわかってからも何とか強くなろうとありとあらゆることをやって鍛えた。そして二十歳の頃には、すごい筋肉がついてボでビルみたいな逆三角形の体になってしまったがその割に技に効果が出ないのでこれではいけないと鍛え方を色々工夫し変えていったのだ。合気のところを強くする鍛え方で、普通の鍛え方とは違う。それでも熱心にならば、普段の私の話の中に鍛え方のヒントのあり気がついてくるはずだ。

Even after I first understood aiki at age 17, I tried all sorts of training regimens to strengthen myself. When I was around 20, I bulked up like an extreme body builder. However, muscle building did not improve my aiki technique. So I had to change my training program. I took a less conventional view and began to explore all kinds of alternatives, innovative regimens that strengthened the aiki and which differed radically from traditional methods. If you're enthusiastic about training, you'll be able to discover it yourself - simply by listening to me you'll notice that I often drop small training hints into my daily conversation.

That's what we're doing here: reconstructing *aiki* conditioning methods from Sagawa's hints.

The ability to mentally control the DLT is the doorway to *aiki* - at least in *conditioning* mode. And the lower body is the key to that door's lock. In combative *application*, obviously other factors will come into play, such as psychology, experience, environment and many other things.

But in this section I'll concentrate on the conditioning side (鍛錬 and 鍛え方) of *aiki*.

If you need further proof that *aiki* is not ordinary physical strength or body tissue or structure, consider the following situation involving Sokaku Takeda, the teacher of Sagawa and apparently the only other 20th century *aiki* master. In the early 1940's, Takeda suffered a sudden severe illness which laid him up in bed, partially paralyzed, unable to walk and barely able to move. He was thought to be within hours of death. He called his adult children and closest students to his bedside, and requested all half dozen or more of them to press down his right arm, each using full strength. He lifted his arm easily against them all, light as a feather. This amazed everybody – no matter how hard they tried to hold him down, his hand came straight up. One of those present said

とても不思議だ。いくら押さえても手が上がってしまう。

It's really weird - no matter how strongly we hold him down, his hand rises right up again.

I'm certain both that this story is true and that it accurately reflects the non-physicality of *aiki* power. I once had my own identical experience at the bedside of a great internal master who was suddenly afflicted with an acute episode of a near-fatal congenital condition and was 'dangerously weak' in exactly this way. You can't believe it until you experience it – in fact you can't believe it even *while* you're experiencing it. Sagawa said:

とくに合気は一種の内部感覚で自得しなければならない

No matter what, you can only get aiki through a particular inner sensation.

This is why I keep saying that although internal power is expressed through the physical, it is inherently something other than physical.

CATCH Core Drill: Extension

Beng Quan (崩拳 bēngquán) is a simple-appearing, walking straight punch, one of the traditional Five Fists (五行拳 wǔxíngquán) of Xingyiquan. My teacher particularly emphasized this as the foundation of Xingyiquan's unique power. In fact, it should be of universal interest, because it functions as an internal power generator like no other. I have covered this extensively in my book *Radical Xingyi Energetics*. Here I'll review those fundamentals but also reset this gem into a new frame, as one of the three core/minimal drills for internal energy work.

External Mechanics

Everybody says *"you can't learn movement arts from a book"*. That's certainly true in this case. Fortunately there are hundreds of Xingyiquan instructional films. All of them cover this technique. My goal here is to unlock the inner activation for you. But we have to get a few externalities in place.

Basically *bengquan* is a stepping straight-forward punch. For best energetic effect, you'll want to do it *aobu* (奥步 áobù) style, which means that your punching hand is always crossed with your lead foot (left/right or right/left) as shown in the illustration. The other way (順步 shùnbù; left/left or right/right) is also possible but in the beginning you won't get the same energy harvest from that. You can work that way later, when you've understood the whole practice.

- Fist is realistically shaped but without tension.
- Shoulders and all upper body relaxed – maintain shape only.
- Head straight, nose always to the center line of motion.
- Turn waist for the physical dynamics of the punch.

Figure 30: In *bengquan*, you step forward and punch mid-level.

- Rear leg takes large step forward, other leg follows just behind.
- Time rear foot placement to finishing instant of punch.
- Body weight 70% on rear foot at finish.

Energetics

Bengquan develops a variety of interesting energetic effects. Once these are experienced, understood, and intensified through this key technique, they can be applied elsewhere in Xingyi practice or in other internal frameworks. The main two effects both derive from the same underlying single internal power, but they feel different in practice, especially for beginners.

Mingjing (明勁 míngjìng 'clear energy') is a short, sharp electric-like bolt of crisp power that flashes through your striking arm(s) at the impact moment of any Xingyiquan technique. The character 明 in this word is the kanji for 'mei' in Sagawa's alternate term for *aiki* power: *transparent power* (透明な力 *toumei na chikara*). In materials on Xingy-iquan, it's common to see *mingjing* mistakenly interpreted as ordinary physical, kinetic, or athletic movement. That is wrong, because *all* martial arts have ordinary kinetic movement. The masters would not need to invent a special term, aligned with the Daoist alchemical powers hierarchy, just for that. Sagawa himself referred to ordinary physical power (used in the athletic martial arts of Judo, Karate, etc.) as 濁った力 (muddy, dirty power) and also as 籠もった力 (hampered, constricted power) - the exact opposite of *mingjing*.

Anjing (暗勁 ànjìng 'hidden energy') is a long, tidal or seismic-feeling wave of power that floods through your entire body from the strong foot to the striking arm(s), just after or simultaneous with the *mingjing* at the impact moment. Beyond these, the great Xingyi masters also talked about *huajing* (化勁 huàjìng), often translated as 'mysterious energy'. Literally however it means 'transformative energy'. This was explained by Guo Yunshen (who trained directly under Li Luoneng, founder of modern Xingyi) as follows:

化勁者。是將暗勁練到至柔至順。
謂之柔順之極處。暗勁之終也。
柔勁之終。是化勁之始也。

Transformative energy arises when you condition the hidden power to be softer and softer, smoother and smoother. When your hidden energy reaches the final extremity of softness and smoothness, it tips over into transformative energy. Transformative energy is the final endpoint of the soft hidden energy. The endpoint of hidden energy overlaps with the starting stage of transformative energy.

Guo arranged these powers in a hierarchy, with the *anjing* arising from the *mingjing*, and the *huajing* arising from transformation of the *anjing*. So we can say that *huajing* arises spontaneously as a *blend* of the two precursor energies. Thus the best rendering of *huajing* is not mysterious energy or even transformative energy, but rather 'blended energy' as indicated by Guo's words above.

The primary word for Sagawa's power is *aiki*, or 合気 in Sino-Japanese. The fundamental meaning of the first character, 合, is to combine, blend, and join. The second character, 気, means energy or power in this context. So the fundamental meaning of *aiki* is also 'blended energy'. Not that words matter all that much, they're just more breadcrumbs on the trail. It's an interesting convergence of concepts.

Anyway, all these powers (clear, hidden, and blended) can be conditioned through the *bengquan* technique, which teaches you to feel, amplify, combine, and finally transcend all three of them.

Fist Closing

One simple way to intensify your experience of both *mingjing* and *anjing* in the technique is to very softly further close your fist at the moment of full extension. I say 'further' because you are using a fist shape throughout the motion of the technique. But it must be a very softly closed fist, with a feeling of emptiness in the center. At the punch's full extension, generate a very slight feeling of softly clenching the fist just a little bit. This will hugely call up the blended power from your feet straight to your fist. It's such a simple trick that I don't have much more to say about it, but it has a profound effect.

∗ ∗ ∗

Fist Angling

If you can feel the power augmentation from the soft closure technique above, you may be ready for an even more powerful augmentation, which is to very slightly *turn up your fist* at the final extension of the punch. It's barely perceptible physically, but seismically powerful energetically. Normally *bengquan* ends with a very slight downward angling of the standing fist's knuckles. Finish that way as normal, but now, at the ending extension, you slightly turn up the lower knuckles a few degrees, flexing at the wrist. This generates at least a triple-power wave of the *anjing* hidden force.

The best mental image to support this technique is to imagine that your striking fist is gripping a very long brush of pencil, held vertically at the end of the punch. The upturn movement is envisioned as drawing or painting a short line on the floor just below your fist, with the imaginary elongated pencil or brush. Naturally, as the upturn is so physically minimal, the resulting line on the floor would be very short. But it's a powerful image that will greatly augment your experience.

✳ ✳ ✳

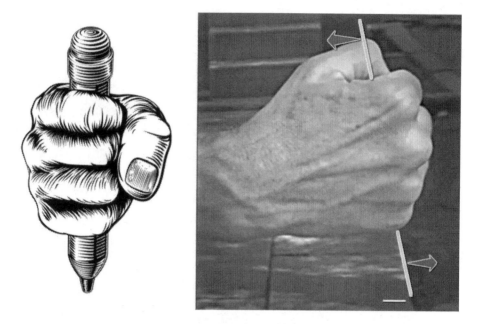

Figure 31: To energize the *anjing* full body wave even further, as you turn up your lower knuckles slightly after the end of the punch, visualize a long pencil or pen, longer than this one (shown), so that its point touches the floor. Use the minimal fist upturn motion to 'draw' a very short line on the floor (in your mind) with the penpoint.

Arrow Concept

Classical Xingyi supermaster Guo Yunshen, and other old-school greats like him, often compared the dynamic of *bengquan* to that of an arrow. The great masters used phrases like: 崩拳如箭 (bēngquánrújiàn; *bengquan is like an arrow*) and 如箭出弦 (rújiànchūxián; *like an arrow coming off the bowstring*), and similar phrases.

There's more to that analogy than meets the eye. At the first and most superficial level, it's obvious that *bengquan* is intended as a straight, fast, level direct punch. Thus at first glance, its motion can definitely be compared to an arrow released from a powerful bow at short range. This is a good image to have when learning the technique and for experiencing the initial lightning bolt of 'clear energy' *mingjing* through the punching forearm and fist.

As you go more deeply into it, you'll be able to merge the various energies. One way to do that is to back up and consider the origin of Xingyiquan. It was originally a military specialty, used in training foot soldiers and spearmen. The military founders of this art knew something about real archery and arrows. The actual trajectory of an arrow in flight is curved. It begins a bit low with some upward angling, peaks in mid flight and bends back down to earth near the target. Of course, if you are shooting arrows (or punching) from three feet away, the full trajectory doesn't matter. It's a straight sucker punch. Still the image of an arrow's actual complete trajectory is extremely useful in extracting the full energetic potential of the technique.

This suggests the mental imagery of Figure 33, the imaginary trajectory for advanced energetic work with *bengquan*.

It's just a suggestive image. In practice you wouldn't make such an obvious and elaborate curve in the punch. You should feel that you are starting a bit 'low', close to *dantian*/hip area, that you slightly rise

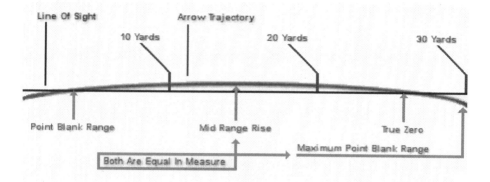

Figure 32: The rise-peak-drop trajectory of an arrow in flight. (crossbowmen.com)

Figure 33: An exaggerated image of the energetically optimal *bengquan* punch trajectory, in line with an arrow's actual flight pattern.

to a 'peak' and that you have a feeling of dropping into the final impact at the end. None of that curvature should be obvious or even visible to an observer, but the inner feeling of it will unleash a great deal more energy potential.

Bengquan Wheel

This leads to the concept of the *bengquan* wheel. If there were a large wheel rim standing on edge, centered at your mid-body, your fist could 'ride' the wheel forward into and through the technique. Your fist would begin just below the top of the wheel, would 'rise' as the wheel rolls forward, and would drop as your elbow thrusts beyond the top of the wheel. In this image, your forearm is 'riding' the wheel forward and the fist arc develops naturally. This feeling of having your forearm 'riding' a wheel that's rolling forward along the floor gives the technique an extremely intense feeling of full body connection. The energy arising from that will flow massively into your forearms and hands on every rep, and also at the end when you stand quietly and collect yourself.

The fist begins at a point just below the top of the wheel, the forearm 'rides' the wheel through the high point of the trajectory, and the fist lowers to the downward endpoint of the trajectory, to finish below the top of the wheel.

You will have to experiment with this to understand it. Remember:

- Your forearm is 'riding' a large wheel forward.
- The wheel is naturally causing the rise-peak-lower trajectory in the fist.

Both of these conditions are powerful aids to relaxation and thus greatly enhance the energetics on every repetition. Your punch execution speed remains rapid and crisp, following standard Xingyi convention. Only the mental/energetic aspect is augmented. Since your punch is riding the wheel, you don't need any strength at all in your arms or shoulders. Your movement is supported by the ground, through the wheel. This has the psychological (and thus energetic) effect of connecting your entire body in motion. It is an extremely powerful training 'secret' – please don't overlook it. Refer frequently to the graphics in this section (the three-position fist curve and the *bengquan* wheel) – this will help your mind.

Figure 34: *Bengquan* supported by an imaginary wheel, depicted just before the final extension of the punch.

NULLIFICATION

I will go down with this ship
And I won't put my hands up and surrender

- Dido (White Flag)

There's another aspect of Sagawa's *aiki* that I haven't yet touched on
- *aiki* for combative application. Sagawa was a supreme martial artist
who easily slammed around anybody who ever stepped up to try him.
He set the 20th century gold standard for the application and deployment of internal martial arts power. Let's hear from him directly for a
high-level description of *aiki* power in use:

私は鍛錬によって力みを捨てた時に本当の力が出てくることを
発見した。

After a lot of intense conditioning, I discovered that when I eliminated all ten-
sion the true power emerged.

合気は技術であり、無力化することである。

Aiki is a technique of nullifying an opponent's force.

敵の力が抜ける（理由を説明した）

I have explained the basis for removal of an enemy's power.

合気は他の武術と違って力でやるわけではないし、敵の力を受けないし、敵の力も出ないようにしてしまう。

Aiki is unlike any other martial technique in that you don't use any physical force at all, nor do you suffer the impact of the enemy's power, because you render him unable to apply any power to you in the first place.

私の合気は外からいくらみても分からない。内部の動きで相手の力を抜いてしまい、形には現れないからね。元は簡単な原理から出発しているのだが誰も気づかない。

You cannot understand my aiki by watching, or from the outside. I have a way of using inner movement to nullify an opponent's force but that part of aiki is invisible. It's based on a simple principle that nobody else happens to have noticed yet.

That last one echoes the key concept of Tai Chi:

此亦意识上之动作不可露形

It is a movement of mind and consciousness, it is not disclosed in physical shape.

There are many other versions of basically the same point (above) throughout the materials on Sagawa. It all begs the question: what conceivable relation does the nullification thing above have to the internal conditioning work we've been going over so far?

To answer that, I'll first need to back up and clear the road of some mud, dirt and debris. When most people talk or think about the possible use of internal power in martial arts, whether skeptic or believe, they are mostly working off the same mistaken premise. It's the fallacious formulation that I call the 'DBZ fantasy'. Dragon Ball Z (DBZ) is a Japanese manga where the characters constantly fight each other with supernatural energy weapons. Geeks on the net talk about the action using this kind of breathless commentary: *... the most massive action during that scene was a ki ball coming at Goku that blows up the planet...*

DBZ is a kids' fantasy cartoon, but it embodies a basic idea of "ki" (quasi-physical internal energy power) as a sort of blast beam or Star Trek Phasers and Photon Torpedoes type of effect. The underlying fallacious concept is that *the energy that moves or damages the target is carried by the impacting beam.*

People who "believe" in internal energy (I don't mean wild-eyed New Age crazies, just people who work the traditional arts in a serious way) hold this idea in the form of traditional 發勁 (fā jìng emitting energy), hoping that if they someday get just the right technique they can blast the enemy off his feet with the directed beam power of their *qi* energy.

At the other end, people who think the whole idea of internal power is a stupid joke (either a laughable mistake based on deplorable physiological ignorance, or a deliberate scam by teachers and cult leaders) naturally deride and reject the above training goal. But what the skeptics are rejecting is the same mistaken concept clung to by the believers. Both parties have a completely wrong idea of it. Whether you're going to work it seriously or debunk it sneeringly, you must at least understand what you're talking about.

The idea that a master can emit an energy effect that on its own power, *in and of itself,* directly moves, damages, or manipulates an opponent's body, is wrong.

It goes without saying that this rules out the 'no contact' hand-waving stuff (though you can use expectation, awe, surprise motions and misdirection tricks to simulate that). It applies equally to contact push hands where people may be hoping someday to blast the partner off his feet directly with a ki ball or power beam of any kind. Not gonna happen.

That said, it is possible for a partner to *perceive* your emitted energy. He can react to it if he so chooses. That need not be fakery, it's an interesting training exercise in itself. But that energy per se is not going to knock a grown man off his feet or up against the wall against his will. That's not what Tai Chi and internal martial arts are about.

So what's the deal then? Are the skeptics right after all? No. There really is an internal martial arts power, but you need to have a more sophisticated understanding of it. Basically the final, visible, physical /kinetic effect of it is all about *him* (your partner/opponent/enemy), not about *you*. There are several modes of use but they all have this same feature: they are about him not you.

In my book *Juice Radical Taiji Energetics*, I discussed the process of *yinjection* at great length. I'm not going over all the details of that again here, but for this discussion I can say that *yinjection* is *triggering* his own inner tension so that he involuntarily uses his own (temporarily uncontrolled) strength to move himself. Aiki *nullification* is the opposite: *removing* his power so that only the barest physical gesture is needed to move him. In neither case is your own energy directly, physically moving him like a blast ray or a tractor beam.

I'll now define "application" as the apparent, superficial, physical correlate of the visible outcome – e.g. a push gesture or whatever – that immediately precedes, and seems to cause, the physical outcome. In Tai Chi's *yinjection*, you must quietly and invisibly *locate and then detonate* his inner tension *before you work your application*. That is the basis of a physically gentle Tai Chi-style "guiding" push gesture being able to uproot a powerful partner. He is uprooting himself. Your energy isn't directly causing it.

In the case of *aiki nullification*, you must quietly and invisibly *take away* his power before you work your application. That is the basis of a physically gentle hand-raising gesture being able to break a strong grip and other such demonstrations.

Both Tai Chi and Daito Ryu have their own fundamental drill to train the skill of nullification. These drills are alike in being widely misunderstood and mostly wasted. In Tai Chi, that drill is called fixed-step push hands and in Daito it is called *te-age* (手上げ pronounced 'tay ah -gay'). When understood correctly, te-age and fixed step push hands are much the same thing. Both can teach nullification, the subject of this chapter.

In *te-age* (TAG from now on), one training partner either stands or sits in *seiza* (on folded legs) with the other partner the same. The 'attacking' partner strongly grips the wrists of the other, pinning his hands and arms either to his sides (standing) or onto his own thighs (seated). The gripped partner tries to raise his hands and free himself. It's a popular drill in Japanese internal martial arts, the subject of many books, DVD's, YouTube videos and magazine articles.

It was through repeated practice of this simple drill that Sagawa came to his *aiki* insight. But notice that even in Sagawa's "sudden" acquisition of his initial *aiki* insight (which I would call his "Aiki Singularity" moment), we can trace the underlying effect of the DLT. Consider how he was practicing. By his own account, he got it initially by repeatedly working the TAG drill, day and night, with his father as his sole training partner.

Consider what's happening in a typical *te-age* scene. The attacker's grip is precisely centered on the *daling* point. And look at the master's responding hands – they are exactly in the Xingyi/DLT configuration, discussed in the previous sections.

I'm won't make too much of this. If Sagawa got his first glimpse of the Aiki Singularity at age 17, it wasn't due to some physical wrist massage or any physical hand shape alone. And I'm generally not a big fan of mechanical interpretations. His breakthrough insight was due to his underlying genius potential meeting up with the right opportunity.

Figure 35: Te-Age (手上げ) Notice the master's relaxed shoulders and also his hands in perfect *daling* throttle (DLT) configuration. That's not a physical technique, it's a way of engaging the internal energy.

And obviously his later mastery of *aiki* went far beyond this narrow *te age* drill setup. Nevertheless, that his initial foundation in the discipline should so precisely track the fundamental training insight of one of the core internal drills is more than merely suggestive. Those who dismiss this as "just a coincidence" are showing they aren't good detectives. A good detective knows that coincidences don't exist.

Most teaching materials pay lip service to Sagawa and the Daito legacy but you'll find the majority are teaching you how to physically game the setup. They advise you on an angle or speed or trajectory to use when raising, cranking or spreading your hands and fingers. They tend to work the letter of the drill (escaping) but not the spirit (nullification). Mostly they teach you some form of redirecting, distracting or overwhelming your partner's strength, but not nullification in the internal sense. I don't blame them though. It's difficult even to understand, much less to actually do or teach. And the internal result looks from the outside very similar to the physical gaming methods – though perhaps a bit smoother and more elegant. But not so different looking, and people want immediate gratification.

Be that as it may, the real nullification happens *before* any physical motion whatsoever. In grappling arts, the wise advise *"position before submission"* - in other words, don't hurry the final clinching move, get him set up right for it first. The counterpart here would be *"nullification before application"*.

If you are contending, even successfully, with his power *as you move*, you have not nullified. Even if you get out, that wasn't *aiki* nullification, it was (perhaps successful) contention and overcoming his force with some combination of your trick and your counter-force. But the point of nullification is that, by the time you begin your physical response, *he should have no power for you to contend with*.

Your application gesture should truly be physically trivial, light and easy. And you shouldn't need any fancy technique either. If a week-old kitten tried to pin your hand down playfully with his paw, would you need a lot of technique, trickiness, strength, angular momentum or any other special secret sauce to get out of it? No, because the kitten is weak relative to you, so you could just gently raise your arm and that's the end of it.

That's the flavor of nullification. The real work is done invisibly before anything physical happens, not as part of the physical response gesture. It may sound woo-woo mystical, but it's a real thing. It's just a technique that's hard to understand, difficult to perform, not particularly practical (at least in the early stages of development), and not widely noticed. Exactly as Sagawa stated.

But this raises questions. For example, how can this nullification technique be trained and what is the relation, if any, of nullification to the internal power conditioning that is described in the rest of this book?

Just as Sagawa's *shiko* is a simple drill framework that allows you to taste the internal effects directly without the distractions of the full Tai Chi form, TAG and fixed-step push hands are both drills that allow you to taste and develop a baby version of nullification without the distractions of full-on sparring, grappling or street fighting. As always, there is a fair chasm between the drill or training versions of nullification vs. the useful application of it in a sportive or street context. But it has enough inherent interest that we can put full-on reality aside for a moment and see what can be done within the training framework.

Nullification is a two-part technique:

1. Clear the circuit
2. Engage the foundation

The two functions can be done simultaneously or in quick sequence. In practice, clearing the circuit boils down to relaxing your shoulders and upper body. You must first be in some kind of contact with your partner, but that should be a very light touch, so you don't block the circuit at the interface.

Now we get to the concepts of "light touch", "butterfly touch" etc. It's the idea that you don't put much or any physical force on people's bodies whether in push hands or healing or whatever modality, so that you remain sensitive to changes and information in their bodies and can easily and flexibly respond. That's all good and a common enough basic idea of all bodywork and martial arts.

To that, I'd like to add something that experienced teachers will understand - but I want to make it explicit. That is the difference between 'touching light' and 'being soft'. They are two related but distinct qualities.

It's surprisingly easy to get people to understand and perform light touch. That's under their conscious control so people immediately understand and mimic well when you tell them 'touch light'. But what is far harder, and something that many instructors cannot themselves perform, is to soften up your touch on your own side. A "light touch" is not necessarily a relaxed hand or body.

If you teach a lot of push hands, you'll find that many people can touch lightly but few can be soft while doing so. Consider a feather vs. a hammer. Both of those can "touch lightly" onto a concrete wall. You can lightly contact the wall surface with a hammer or feather such that barely even four ounces would be felt. But that does not address the inherent nature of the hammer vs. the feather themselves, on the inside. You can touch lightly with a hammer, even caress with it (as in movies when the villain caresses the captive beauty's face ever so lightly and sinisterly with a knife, gun barrel, or icepick). But that's not the deepest essence.

It may seem like a difference that makes no difference. The masking of intent, a "light touch" - whether "soft" or not - usually can get the job done on most people, tense as they typically are. But true relaxation requires a deeper analysis. No matter how much the Classics talk about absolute relaxation, *most people are still way too tense in their hands and arms*. Our minds and our culture have made us up-tight like that. The initial nullification touch requires no physical tension. At the same time, we can't let the hands and arms go totally slack and die, that's not Tai Chi relaxation either.

There are two kinds of nerves: afferent and efferent. Here's a summary of the distinction:

Neurons that receive information from our sensory organs (e.g. eye, skin) and transmit this input to the central nervous system are called afferent neurons. Neurons that send impulses from the central nervous system to your limbs and organs are called efferent neurons.

Therefore, as the afferent neurons convey the sensory stimulus to the brain (like the burning sensation of a candle), the efferent neurons convey the motor stimulus to the muscles (moving the hand away from the candle). To sum it up: Afferent = Receive and Efferent = Act.

One extremely important key to internal energy training is based on a working/training level awareness of this feeling vs. acting distinction. This doesn't mean the internal energy is inherently physiological, as many wish it could be. But it's a useful concept that can pay cash for internal training. So you pretend in your mind that your hand, and in fact the entire wrist and forearm, have no motor nerves – that only sensory nerves are present.

Your hands and wrist and forearms can still *feel* - but they cannot *act*. You have full afferent or sensory nervous structure and activation paths in your arms but you have no efferent or motor system at all in those regions. If you (imagine that you) have no motor pathways, then you can't tense or over-manipulate. Though soft, your arms become like 'dead' things, a wooden short staff or a peg leg. But actually they are only half-dead... undead? They remain intensely aware and sensitive in your mind alone. They are acutely receptive to the slightest touch of the lightest zephyr of breeze, or the brush of a fly's wing. This concept can be used in both partner and solo training.

Once you've applied the correct touch, whole-body relaxation clears the rest of the circuit, all the way down. Down to what? Down to your *foundation*.

> **Engaging the foundation means flashing your mind down to whatever part of your body is in contact with the supporting surface.**

The foundation could be your feet (standing), your butt (sitting), your shins (*seiza*), etc. Just the fact of doing this will momentarily 'vacuum in' your partner's power. Then and only then, you may make your application gesture to close the interaction.

But you have to take relaxation seriously. If you won't take my advice, consider the words of Sagawa again, talking about his teacher Sokaku Takeda:

武田先生も完全然力んでいないかった。力んでいたら効かないよ。ススーと力まずに出ていた。他の弟子は先生の手の強さや重さばかりに気を取られてそういうことは気付かなかったかもしれない。力んだらそこで力が止まってしまう。それは単に自己満足に過ぎない。

Takeda sensei was always absolutely relaxed. If he'd used strength nothing he did would have worked. The other students were so impressed by the power and weight of sensei's hands that they failed to notice this deeper thing. If you use any physical strength your power is immediately cut off. Using strength is merely self-delusion.

It's simple to describe and not so hard to do – under ideal conditions. Unfortunately *conditions are rarely ideal*. All kinds of things can break down the idealized nullification technique. Situational and time pressures, intimidation, inattention, fear, pride, attention-seeking, and other emotions can distract you enough to prevent pristine application of the nullify technique.

And there's another factor, which gets to the link between the nullification technique and the internal conditioning work.

> **Nullification works better the more internal current you have built up through your solo conditioning (shiko, Tai Chi, Santishi, etc.)**

In fact, the ARC process is very closely aligned with the nullification circuit. Let's look at where these two seemingly disparate concepts touch.

The A in ARC stands for accumulate. Listed synonyms for 'accumulate' include terms such as: *gather, draw in,* and *collect.* When you work the solo ARC practices, the accumulation takes in feedstock of nutrition, light, sound, air, and other physical and energetic constituents of our world and somehow (nobody knows how) transduces them to the internal power I've been discussing. The nullification technique is essentially an extension of this accumulation process.

By emptying yourself of tension under contact conditions, and providing that mentally activated foundation as a 'sink' for the energy, you draw in his physical power momentarily and transduce it to something that is naturally drawn to your foundation. It's comparable to a kind of grounding (by analogy with electricity, not the structural 'groundpath' concept normally discussed on the internet as a kinetic and structural function). So the two branches of internal work fit together.

Note carefully that the 'emptying' step of nullification is not the common Tai Chi push-hands trick of a very slight, almost imperceptible physical withdrawal of your body (while keeping hands in contact) to lure and game your partner, followed by a quick hard shove as he leans into you in response. That will work most of the time, and it's fine as far as it goes. But it isn't what I'm talking about here. That is a mechanical and structural trick, but the nullification is truly an invisible inner energetic process. Transparent, if you will. Anyway that physical withdrawal trick won't work with seated TAG practice, because your hands are pressed hard to your thighs.

This isn't a deep explanation of how it works. It's only functional notes. But it's adequate to begin practice. You don't need a doctorate in Hilbert's formalist foundations of pure mathematics to work the technique of long division. Long division is real and workable, but due to your own limitations you won't get the right answer every single time – and whatever can be said of long division applies to nullification practice. But as with anything else, practice may someday make perfect. I'm not saying I'm any great master of this. I have my ups and downs with it. As the Preacher said: *"time and chance happeneth to them all"*. I'm more of a reporter than anything else. I'm telling you what I've found to be real and interesting to work on, nothing more.

It sounds too easy, doesn't it? You "think his power down"? Well, yes and no. It's not physically hard to practice this technique. The hard part is psychological and emotional. The big barriers are fear and pride. It's super difficult for people to let go of upper-body resistance and *trust their foundation*. That's why few ever get near this "simple principle". It's too scary to drop the arm and shoulder tension and trust that the circuit and foundation will nullify the other guy.

Sagawa stated that when he was first exposed to martial arts training, through his father's involvement with Sokaku Takeda, he wasn't all that thrilled or interested. However, for some reason the TAG drill intrigued him, so he worked intensely on that with his father and came to understand the nullification technique. Later he became quite engrossed in developing the power further. But it may be that Sagawa first understood *aiki* precisely because he was not originally so into martial arts and combatives. That may have freed up his mind and body enough to let something happen.

The difficulty is overcoming our fear and aggression. The hardest thing is relaxing and taking that crucial instant to 'nullify before apply'. When you enage your foundation with your mind, the power drain seems to happen automatically. You only need to set up the right conditions in a timely fashion (before he blasts you). But there's the real challenge – making it work invariantly under all conditions with non-compliant partners. That *is* a serious challenge, for me and everybody else.

How similar to each other are Tai Chi's push hands and Daito's *te-age* (TAG)? Very similar, below the surface:

1. They're both finely crafted frameworks for learning nullification.
2. They're both artificial and inapplicable as such to any 'real' combative scenario.

The big difference between them is that TAG seems to be accepted at face value as a practice drill, or a learning game. Fixed-step push hands, on the other hand, is subject to wild and almost crazy misunderstanding and is totally overloaded with ridiculous misconceptions from all directions. The appearance of push hands seems to freak people out. I guess it looks enough like fight training to over-excite some people, yet not quite enough like a 'real' fight to avoid irritating others. It's in a freaky martial arts Twilight Zone. But when you forget the fight, all becomes clear.

People may have a little ego when working TAG, but few take it as anything other than an amusing educational game. When it comes to push hands, for some reason there's an underlying edge to it, as though people want to interpret it as combative encounter or test. This comes out a lot with fixed-step push hands. If my partner has trouble moving me with the simple push-hands drill as specified (essentially it's no more "specialized" or "exotic" a practice than holding down somebody's hands), most people with martial arts background immediately escalate to punches or full-on grappling, throwing, sweeping, or whatever. Even rabbit punches, head-butts and ear chomps ala Holyfield v. Tyson are possible. When unable to handle the basic drill, they quickly ramp up other elements. People would rather flip the board than lose the game.

That isn't necessarily a bad thing. Though it sometimes results in a few bruises for me, I don't really mind all that much. It can be interesting to see what they come up with, and it's potentially a good training opportunity. But I generally resist the urge to counter-escalate. I do have my backlist of combative skills beyond fixed step push hands, derived from boxing and other things. In other activities I've dished out more than my share of dislocated jaws, black eyes, doubled-over liver shots and blood all over the canvas. But in fixed-step push hands I rarely counter-escalate.

What's the point? If I'm unable to nullify their escalations, I just ride the throw or whatever they want to do to me, shake hands and we're done. I view that as my partner's missed opportunity to really work the drill deeply, his failure to recognize that it's not in any way a realistic fight scenario but that it has something profound to teach. My partner, on the other hand, leaves shaking his head at how deluded I am to focus on such an "unrealistic" fight practice. Just another multi-cultural moment.

I resonate with what Tai Chi teacher Koh Ah-Tee said in an interview about his push-hands encounter with famous old-time Tai Chi master Huang Xingxian:

When I was pushing hands with Huang Hsing Hsien and he was unable to push me over, he started to hit me. I pointed out to him that this was dangerous and that I too could do the same to him.

Verbal de-escalation like that is my preferred approach also. It's meaningless to treat push hands as more than a drill. Nobody tries to escalate TAG and neither should push hands ever be escalated (unless both partners agree to a specific drill change). Once you start down the road of unilateral and then bilateral escalation, there's no end to the number and types of fight tricks that could be applied.

The quote above about "going down with the ship" and "not surrendering" does not mean what you may think. It does not mean that I fight bitterly to avoid losing the game, using my boxing or head-butting. ear-biting, rabbit punches, knee grabs, sweeps, trips, throws and foot stomps, etc. It means that, despite every failure and imperfection, I will never knowingly compromise the higher goal of eschewing physical force, weight, mass, strength, and technique. I'd rather "lose" than cheat on the beautiful ideal of nullification. To go down with the ship means to invest in loss, as Professor Zheng taught us.

There are several specific sub-configurations within fixed step push hands that particularly lend themselves to experiencing and developing nullification skill.

Defensive Nullification

Using the word 'defense' doesn't mean it's a fight. It means that you take away his strength while he's actively attempting to apply it to you. In this mode, you do not push, you await your partner's push. Keeping light contact with any part of his body creates the circuit. Engaging your foundation (feet in this case) with your mind nullifies his push.

That's it. You took away his power, therefore his push isn't strong enough to move you. I know it should sound more complicated, but if you do those two things over time you'll become nearly immovable. Not that being immovable has much practical fight value, but you can learn something about the inner energetics of nullification. It's exactly analogous to the equally 'unrealistic' TAG experience.

Offensive Nullification

The 'offensive' mode works exactly the same way, except that now he awaits your 'push'. I put 'push' in quotes because if you do it right, all he's going to feel is an empty push gesture, not a physical shove. Touch very lightly to set up the circuit, and just prior to initiating your physical gesture, again engage your foundation (your feet in this case) with your mind, then lightly move your hands right through him. Since you have taken away his power in advance of your move, make sure your gesture is never strong enough to physically move him. You don't need that much power. You took away his physical strength to resist, so momentarily you need no more physical strength to knock him back than you would use to topple an upright-balanced 2x4 stick of lumber. If you feel any resistance from him, it means you didn't fully nullify him prior to making your gesture.

Translating the above nullification skill to broader and more varied situations against more aggressive and stronger partners is a tremendous creative challenge, and a lifetime's work. But nullification technique is where it begins.

Comeback Nullification

Nullification as so far discussed is mostly concerned with merging his physical power into your Accumulate (and drop-to-dissipate) phase of the ARC. Concomitant with the ARC model though, there's also Rebound and Catch (bringing back up to hands). For basic nullification you don't need to concern yourself with those elements. Once his power is taken away, you can "use his weakness" to topple him. However, it is instructive to sometimes "use his strength" to topple him. One way to do that is via the yinjection process discussed in detail in *Juice*.

Another way is to build on the nullification, and rather than simply dissipating his incoming energy into the ground, bounce it (Rebound it) up from your feet to your hands and quickly toss it back on to him. Again the focus is never on *your* anything, it's only returning *his* power. It would be nice to have more detailed instruction, elaborate procedures and scientific proof (or at least practical evidence). But it really is as simple to play with as what I've written here. Remember what Sagawa said *"...a simple principle that nobody has noticed"*. The two steps of nullification are all you need to get started.

The hard part isn't finding a lot complicated details on the exact internal procedure. The hard part for all of us in this is overcoming our own fear, ego, pride, anger and other psych issues that render us unable to take the chance of letting go of our own protective strength and aggression.

The Big Picture

Lurking behind all this is the usual existential problem: why? Even if you could develop this perfectly, to Sagawa's level or beyond, what would be the ultimate value? I talked a lot about this in my book *Juice* so I won't repeat all that. The practical value of even total mastery of unarmed combat is limited, except in a marginal economic sense (maybe try for UFC? Maybe become a famous seminar teacher or YouTube demonstrator? Or possibly work in executive protection).

It is said that Tai Chi founder Zhang Sanfeng could levitate (a skill beyond even the proudest internal masters of the present day) yet a guy with a 12-gauge could blast him out of the sky like a skeet, trap or clay target. I've already opined in *Juice* that the technologically un-augmented and non-weaponized human body is fast becoming obsolete. Therefore, no matter what level of skill is attained, this internal cultivation is mostly a boutique hobby activity – yet still, a fascinating historical pursuit, like blacksmithing or wooden boat building.

But one potentially useful attribute, does grow out of this work. That is the development of extreme sensitivity, leading to the quality that I call *automaticity*. Automaticity is my word for the supreme goal of martial arts training, which is to respond to any threat from any direction instantaneously without even seeing or hearing. The great internal master Sun Lutang described this:

不動之時。內中寂然。空虛無一動其心。至於忽然有不測之事。雖不見不聞。而能覺而避之。

Abiding without motion, steeped in perfect inner stillness, empty with an immovable mind, when there's a sudden threat, even if unseen and unheard, the master avoids it as though he knew it was coming. Before it appears to the senses, he has already known it.

The best example of this was the founder of modern Xingyiquan, Li Nengran (Luoneng).

本境有某甲。武進士也。體力逾常人。兼善拳術。與先生素相善。而於先生之武術。則竊有不服。每蓄意相較。輒以相善之故。難於啟齒。一日會談一室。言笑一如平常。初不料某甲之蓄意相試。毫無防備之意。而某甲於先生行動時。乘其不意。竊於身後即捉住先生。用力舉起。及一伸手。而身體已騰空斜上。頭顱觸入頂

棚之内。復行落下。兩足仍直立於地。未嘗傾跌。以邪術疑先生。先生告之曰。是非邪術也。蓋拳術上乘神化之功。有不見不聞之知覺。故神妙若此。非汝之所知也。時人遂稱先生曰。神拳李能然

In that region there was a man who was very skilled in the military arts, and whose strength and prowess were truly outstanding. He was on good terms with Li, but he harbored serious reservations about how skilled the master really was. He always liked to try out people's skill for real, but since Master Li was a friend, he couldn't bring himself to challenge him. But one day when the two of them were together, chatting and joking around as usual, the man suddenly decided to go for it. Without any warning, hoping to catch Li off-guard, he rushed from behind to seize the master in a crushing bear hug, attempting to lift him off his feet. But as soon as he extended his arms, he found himself blasted straight up through the ceiling of the room. He then felt himself floating down gently to the floor below. He suspected Li of witchcraft, but Li told him that this kind of unconscious perception was not sorcery; it was simply the peak of the boxing art.

Rock star. Anyway, the more of this highly restricted fixed-step push hands and/or TAG work you do, the greater your Automaticity Quotient (AQ) grows. Sagawa had that in full measure:

駅で我々が降りようとした時、ヤクザ風の体格の良い男がいきなり乗り込んできて先生に体当たりを喰わそうとした。私は１.５メートル位離れていてとつさのことにあ！と思った瞬間、先生はサッと体を横へ買わされその男はまるで突っかい棒が取れたように座席へワット倒れ、びっくりした顔で先生の方を見ていた。先生はまた何気なく元の位置にもどり何事もなかったかのように電車を降りた。

When we got off the train a big muscular gangster type of guy suddenly crashed in and tried to bash into the teacher. I was several feet away with no time to do anything but I saw the teacher take a quick side-step. The man smashed

into the row of seats at the side of the doors, as though somebody had kicked out a stick propping him up. He gaped at the teacher with blank surprise. But the teacher just resumed his place at the doors and got off the train without a trace of fluster.

I have the baby version of this ability. Occasionally in Japan or China, on the trains and subway, a certain kind of tough guy who dislikes foreigners will attempt a sudden shoulder smash as he walks by. Just a little micro-aggression to put us in our place. It doesn't happen often but it happens. However, although over the years a fair number of such toughs have attempted this with me, it has never succeeded. It's fun to see them stumble and lurch an awkward stutter-step as my shoulder or body 'moves on its own' at just the instant of pre-contact. Oops, nothing there! It's not a conscious thing on my part, I merely enjoy glimpsing the comical and confused aftermath.

That's very far from what Master Li and Sagawa were doing, but it's a baby step at the starting gate on the same road. If Li Nengran achieved the maximal AQ of let's say 100, my AQ would be 3 or so. But if you've never done the kind of nullification training I'm talking about here, your AQ might be only 1 or 2. So get going on it.

But no matter how much push-hands, TAG, *kuzushi* (standup grappling and unbalancing), or other partner work you do, the internal conditioning is always paramount. Sagawa said:

崩しは合気の一部だが、全てではない。それと鍛錬だ。鍛錬していても合気を取りにくいのに、鍛錬していないものがわかるはずはない。

Kuzushi is a part of aiki training, but it isn't the whole thing. The other key is internal conditioning. Even if you do a lot of internal conditioning, it's still hard to get the skill of aiki. But without that, there's little chance you'll ever understand aiki at all.

CONCLUSION

My friends in Brazilian ju-jitsu and boxing would regard this whole book as an entertaining fantasy. They hold very reasonably to the idea that martial skill does not arise from mysterious powers, nor does it happen overnight. It's the result of decades of hard-ass, sweat-soaked mat and ring time against hard and seriously committed fellow athletes. It's the gradual accumulation of instinct and movement expertise under high-pressure situations, seasoned with never-ending, always-escalating daily physical conditioning. This is a state-of-the-art sports science view of the physical and psychological aspects of skill development However, that gradual development emphasis, which we might call the "evolutionary model" does not account for how a scrawny, sickly 17 year-old teen, with nobody but his dad for a training partner, working the most limited and absurdly unrealistic of drills, pierced the innermost mystery of martial arts.

Meanwhile, my Tai Chi, Qi Gong and Aikido friends will likewise regard this book as fantasy, but from the opposite angle. In their world, *aiki* and *jing* and such inner powers are thought to be real enough, but those powers and experiences are regarded as so remote, exotic and exalted that there's no way an average Joe like me, who is gradually developing and refining them with many stutter steps over time, could possibly have any insight. In their view, if I really had access to these powers, I should have been surrounded by a golden light and instantly become absolutely undefeatable. So under this "revolutionary model", I must be just a talker and faking it all. This line of thought does not account for Sagawa's emphasis on long-term training, on the decades of time and unending work required to keep growing in the art. Sagawa said:

合気が分かってから本当の修行が始まるのだ。長い間の持続した鍛錬と研究の結果。少しずつできるようになってくるものだ。

It's only after you understand aiki that the real training can begin. You come to master it gradually, little by little, over a long period of conditioning and personal research.

> **The Aiki Singularity is not the finish line, it's the starting gun.**

Anyway, there's merit in both the above views. But both lines are missing something. That missing something is the gap that this book has tried to fill. And as long as I have an even marginally functional body and mind, I'll never give up the internal power pursuit. No matter what kind of setbacks, embarrassments, internet shout-downs or single-star attack reviews I have to endure, no matter how dismally over-owned, over-engineered or radioactively toxic our world becomes, I'll never compromise my pursuit of the true internal art. I'll carry on as a 'party of one' to the end – even if I never become a UFC cage-beast. I will go down with this ship.

So now it's your call. Give it a shot and let me know sometime how it goes.

APPENDIX A: JADE PILLOW

Professor Zheng wrote as follows:

练纯熟时自有气从背脊骨直往劲顶上冲越玉枕而达百会复下降丹
田

My translation:

When you're really rocking it, the qi energy automatically surges up the spine from the sacrum, directly ascending through the spinal column, then traversing the jade pillow point and surmounting the crown center before plunging back to the dantian below.

I've described some of the energy architecture and hotspots of the body in my books, singling out a few of the centers as particularly relevant for beginners. Now I'll discuss one that I haven't called much attention to earlier: the Jade Pillow（玉枕 yùzhěn）point on the lower rear of the skull, which Professor Zheng refers to in the line above.

First I want to explain why I haven't gotten into this before. Although the *traversal of the jade pillow* is an amazing and fully tangible, fully 'real' and concrete occurrence at a certain stage of training, it has to emerge organically. Sometimes if a writer emphasizes a point, everybody gets too tensely and expectantly conscious of that point. That kind of mind delays things. The traversal of the jade pillow isn't something you *do*, it's something that *happens* by itself.

You can feel a lot of energy and have all kinds of experiences over a long period without yet having this Jade Pillow traversal (JPT) thing. But it's important and eventually it will happen. Although the JPT phenomenon is the result of accumulated practice, the actual moment of traversal begins distinctly and clearly. At some point while doing the ZMQ form or holding one of its poses, you'll suddenly become aware of a rhythmic tapping press, a little mini thumping, at the lower rear of your skull just below the occipital ridge.

I could get into a whole matchup thing of the traditional expression (yùzhěn) with the finely detailed network of traditional Chinese medicine's acu-points. But that isn't necessary. The acu-points are highly detailed because they deal with needles. For energy work, the results manifest more in a zone of the energy body than in a pinpoint of the physical body. So location-wise the description given should suffice.

However non-physical the underlying energy architecture may be, you will feel a physical effect when the JPT begins. This is subtle but unmistakable. Imagine one of those reflex hammers, used by doctors on your knee. Now imagine the head of such a hammer wrapped with thick cotton, packed tight onto the small hammer head. Someday you'll be practicing the Tai Chi form and you'll experience the feeling of such a hammer very gently 'tapping' on the indicated spot. This tapping will seem to originate from directly below the target spot. IT isn't something you consciously work to create. It begins spontaneously.

Within a matter of days or even hours, the 'tapping' will speed up and get stronger and faster, stronger and faster, and finally it will become an unbroken stream through the gate of the yùzhěn. The power will flood through your head and light up every head point, not just the crown point that often gets special attention. The power will flood through and illuminate the niwan, the yintang (points I've covered in books) and even the side areas around your ears - everywhere.

At that stage, it's still limited to the realm of sedentary meditation effects, like the micro-cosmic orbit or *neidan* type of work. What makes it Tai Chi, a truly transcendent form of practice, is that the power will then surge from the center brain point (*niwan*) down your front (*yin-tang*; forehead and beyond) and through your arms. That is when the real Tai Chi fun begins. No matter how much internal flow power you had felt before the JPT event, the arm flow will be 10x that, or more like 100x, afterwards.

When the internal power is gated in the above way explicitly through the *yuzhen*, it is like the sluice gate in a big dam. That is, while an un-dammed river has more raw volume, the flow through the sluice gate is far more powerful in psi and velocity than the natural river current. It's a fascinating effect.

Appendix B: Tai Chi Mahamudra

A key concept and practice in yoga is the *mahamudra*. This is defined by Wiki as follows:

Pressure is exerted with the heel on the perineum (Muladhara Chakra). This zone is considered to be closely involved in the control of the vital potential. At the same time, the throat is compressed (Jalandhara Bandha) activating the throat chakra (Vishuddha Chakra) - center of the akashic energies of void. By activating the energies of akasha and simultaneously stimulating the energies of Muladhara Chakra, Kundalini awakens and raises through the central channel, Sushumna Nadi. The void is considered to be a substrate, an intermediary state in any transformation. Here it projects the lower energies up the spine, transforming them to spiritual energies instead. Thus Mahamudra is a gesture of alchemical transformation, and at the same time a method of awakening of the supreme energy of the body, Kundalini.

The description above mentions the Jalandara Bandha, which is the throat lock:

Jālandhara bandha comes from Sanskrit. Jāla means web or "net" and dhara means "holding". Bandha means "bond; contracting". It is performed by extending the neck and elevating the sternum (breastbone) before dropping the head so that the chin may rest on the chest.

This is a highly spiritual discipline and also therapeutic yoga practice. It both assumes and requires a very different approach to energetic

Figure 36: Yoga supermaster Krishnamacharya peforming Mahamudra. Note the chin or throat lock, Jalandara Bandha.

cultivation than the framework of this book. But there is a Tai Chi version of Mahamura and Jalandara Bandha that is a supremely interesting and powerful energy practice. I will call it TCB, for 'Tai Chi Bandha'. The TCB is advanced work. If you are not yet feeling the various energy phenomena described in the main sections of this book, don't jump into this. It's *not dangerous* at all, but you will simply frustrate yourself by trying to run before you can walk.

I am fully aware of the 'authentic yoga version of Mahamudra. I have practiced Ashtanga Yoga First and Second Series (including a full set of Pranayama, where the *Bandha* are most emphasized) under the tutelage of a direct lineage holder – straight, uncut, from the Continent. The Ashtanga *pranayama* and *asana* are fantastic practices. But they do not allow you to work as directly with the energy pressure currents as Tai Chi does, simply because most people are so deliberately tense, stretched, twisted and distracted by the strict and forceful breathing regimen that they have no bandwidth left to notice the arising of the soft internal power.

If you're into yogic *bandha* practice , please continue with that. This is something different and it doesn't conflict with yoga in any way. I wanted to mention the superficial resemblance, though, because the energetic result of the TCB tracks very well onto the mythical (but rarely attained) energetic highs described in the yoga classic writings.

The time to begin TCB experimentation is when, during the Inner Activated version of the Santishi (see 'ACCUMULATE Core Drill') you *naturally* begin to notice an extremely soft feeling of pressure under your lower jaw, as you stand. It begins so subtly that at first you should find yourself questioning whether anything is happening at all. It may first become noticeable as soft waves 'lapping' very gently at the underside of your jaw and upper neck. Over time, the soft pressure will become a more constant and definite current.

From the performance of all the work in this book (not only the Santishi of course), the energy of your trunk is becoming so full and strong that it has 'filled' you to the point of near overflow. That's not a bad thing at all. You can work with it more precisely now. You should continue all other practices (or at least, the ones you have found enjoyable and effective). But if you want to pursue this avenue of deepening the energetic experience, here's something amazing you can do.

The posture I use for going deeper with TCB is *Single Whip*. Any other ZMQ37 pose will do. You can use any of the seven poses described and illustrated in my book *Tai Chi Peng: Root Power Rising*. Here I'll use Single Whip for illustration. Single Whip is one of only two practices that Professor Zheng ever witnessed his own teacher Yang Chengfu performing in his own practice, as his own private work.

Start with a correct configuration of the 70/30 (front-weighted) Tai Chi pose Single Whip. All the normal Tai Chi requirements apply: relax, body upright, Fair Lady's hand in the front, relaxed wrist for the side hook hand, etc. For this practice, I will assume you've picked up the basics of ZMQ37 poses from my other books.

If you have begun to notice the under-chin pressure (as above) then it will be extremely natural for you to depress your jaw very slightly, and very minimally pull your head and neck back. This is emphatically NOT the tightly clamped, physical high-pressure lock of the yoga Jalandara Bandha (see the master's photo above).

You're working with an energy mass here, between the top of your sternum and lower throat as the lower edge, and the underside of your jaw as the upper edge. Imagine you are very gently holding a soft baseball, like a nerf-ball, under your chin. Just enough pressure is exerted to keep the ball in place, no more. You will actually feel the energetic mass there. An outside observer should barely be able to notice any change or dramatic lowering and retracting of your head or chin. It's a centimeter or less, mostly mental. Feel the energy with the underside of your jaw using the same mental sensitivity that you would apply to feeling a soft cloth or fur with your hands.

The power is gigantic, but your physical 'grip' on it at its edges is soft and delicate. The energy is coming from inside your throat but it will feel as though it's projecting outside as well. We're controlling the edge of the power softly, like an elite hunting dog that retrieves a downed duck in his jaws, bearing it gently to the hunter without leaving a single dent in the duck from its fangs, mouthing the bird's carcass delicately with the barest edges of teeth.

But TCB doesn't stop with that. That is the 'minor range' – from jaw
to sternum. The 'major range' is the area between the jaw area and
the hip joints. I've been talking a lot about the hips in this book so you
should be energetically sensitized to them by now. Mentally feel that
you are gently holding, trapping or compressing another, much larger
mass of internal energy, which will fill your torso strongly, as long as

you keep this 'lock' in place. Thus the lower hip joints (or inguinal crease if that's easier to visualize) act as the lower boundary in place of the *Muladhara* of yoga's *Mahamudra* (see above). Just as a dam does not fully block, but rather concentrates a river's power, so this torso 'lock' effect massively energizes your arms, hands, legs, and feet.

Remember it is not tense and physical like the yoga locks. You don't even need much mental exertion to feel it and intensify it. As long as you keep the gentle chin lock, and the hip / inguinal consciousness, the power will crystallize throughout your trunk. Don't worry about theoretical stuff - serpentine spinal currents, or which direction the cosmic the flow is supposed to be running, or any of that arcana. Just feel the power, surf it, it's great.

You will realize that in the TCB, we are substituting the hip creases as the lower bound of the lock, instead of the perineum (*Muladhara*) plugged by your heel as in yoga. This is physically gentler and energetically smoother, eliminating the danger of uncontrolled kundalini eruption through the spine. In TCB, the energy is not narrowly channeled through the spinal *nadi*, but is spread throughout the trunk, much like the Old Ox Power phenomenon mentioned earlier.

I'm taking a chance by providing this Appendix. After all, it is written in the *Hatha Yoga Pradipika* (classic Sanskrit manual on hatha yoga) as follows:

This Maha Mudra is the giver of great powers (Siddhi) to men. It should be kept secret by every effort, and not revealed to any and everyone.

But what the hell. When you're ready for it, now you know how to work it.

Appendix C: Crafting Your Perfect 1-Star Review

You know the importance of producing the very best 1-star book review you're capable of. I don't need to remind you why. We all know that online shoppers' eyes glaze over at a mountain of 5-stars, but they'll eagerly seek out and ravenously devour a single lonely 1-star. So there's your ego boost right there: *people will read your stuff*! But it gets better.

Because even if an online shopper should happen to accidentally glance at a word or so of a more positive review (2+ stars), *they won't believe a word of it.* They'll quite naturally assume it was written by the author's mom or his publisher, or that the author has paid some SEO scumbag to grind out zombie fakes on demand. But your 1-star, on the other hand - no matter whether you're a competitor, an enemy, a troll, a liar, a fake, an idiot, whatever - will be reverently attended like the Delphic Oracle. So it pays to take the time to hone your craft - The Art of the One-Star Review.

And I'm going to help you with that. I'll use this very book as a stalking horse to illustrate the teachings, *'without loss of generality'* as they say in higher mathematics. After trashing this book for practice, you can get out there and hunt bigger game. Before we get going though, I need to set you up with a few preliminaries (my course in Crafting Your Perfect

1-Star Review does not graduate cripples!). Here are the pre-requisite considerations:

(i) **Targeting:**

Generally you are best off firing your 1-star at fictional works, such as novels. That's because novels are more 'of a piece' than instructional non-fiction books (such as this present work). Novels are like ocean water, where the salt is uniformly dissolved and distributed. Instructional books are chunkier, like a stew, and it would be surprising if there were nothing at all, *nothing whatsoever*, that you could learn from an instructional book of reasonable size. Remember the bold claim that gives the 1-Star its unique power – the idea that the book in question is so bad that there is *nothing* to be gained from it *whatsoever*, that it has absolutely *no* redeeming qualities. So once you've fully mastered 1-star review writing, fiction is generally your best hunting ground - but you can certainly use this present non-fiction book for target practice.

(ii) **Logic:**

You use the 1-star to project your disgust and fervent wish that the system would allow you to award even fewer stars - zero or negative numbers. Don't make an idiot of yourself by actually admitting that you *did* get something from it, as one reviewer did with a certain other author's martial arts book (not mine). The righteously outraged reviewer grudgingly gave it 1 star (so far so good), but then asserted that the work was completely useless... *"except for two of Wang Xiang Zhai's special techniques. One technique for finding hidden places of tension or blockage, and the other is Wang Xiang Zhai's therapeutic health postures that I have been looking for, for some time."* Please. There the reviewer was, rolling along, slashing and burning, fervently justifying his outrage and hate and all we 1-star aficionados and believers were rocking it right along with him, totally grooving on the ride, and then – we're brought up short with that? What a buzzkill! How can you maintain your 1-Star dread-cred when you say something like *that*, which obviously puts the book at 2+ stars? *"looking for, for some time..."* (Though this reviewer *does* score high on originality and creativity for his unprecedented observation that the book in question was *"a huge disappointment"* – you sure don't see *that* in every single 1-star review ever written...).

(iii) **Timing:**

It's important to get your 1-star up on the system as soon as possible after the target book first appears. Don't give readers the impression that you needed time to ponder, work with, understand and digest the material. Think how brilliant you'll appear with a flash review – in no time flat you instantly grokked the book's complete worthlessness! That's really incisive perception. So don't dawdle, grind it out and get it up.

If you've absorbed the preliminaries, here are some lines of ready-made boilerplate to consider for use in your 1-star review of this book:

"too many jokes"

This is always a nice general-purpose hammer in your critical toolkit. Unfortunately you can't use it to slam this particular book. There are no jokes in this book. Please redirect fire to *Juice Radical Taiji Energetics* instead.

"too many acronyms, made up his own language"

Yes! This is a great one. It's always good to discourage originality and a fresh take on a known topic. Problem is that in this particular book, unlike the prior book *Juice*, there are no acronyms (there *are* a few abbreviations, but that's leaner meat).

"nothing but recycled blog posts"

Ah! One of the best lines of attack when you have nothing else to say. The great thing about this one is that it manages to spin the author's previous gift to the world of *original free-of-charge* content and turn that into a negative. So definitely go for it. It's a fair and honorable point to emphasize. Be sure to stress that you got *no value whatsoever* from the substantial re-writing, editing, thematic re-organization, etc. – and be very, very quiet about the 90% of this book's material that's totally fresh or a radical extension. Ignore that the book provides a chance to learn more from a fresh and deeper view of the core material. I can only advise you generically here however, because, while the contents of this particular book you're holding in your hands may have in some cases been originally inspired by reader questions that were addressed in my blog, everything has been so substantially re-written and expanded and unified that it might as well be all new material.

"not enough drills"

This is a great one. Who wants to buy a hamburger only to find it's just a chunk of lettuce and a tomato slice? Where's the meat? (Although maybe somebody can explain to me the obsession with *quantity*, why it's necessarily good to always grab for *more* drills – do you have more than 24 hours in your day? What you actually need are *fewer* drills, the *right* drills, the ones that *work best* – that's the real service a book should provide). Anyway, yeah. You could say this. Unfortunately, you'd be lying. There are lots of illustrated drills in this book, enough for a lifetime of work. That pretty much takes down your standard "not enough drills" attack like an IRA power drill through the kneecap. But it was a good try, an insightful line of approach, don't get discouraged.

"so full of himself"

Finally here's some pay dirt! You just have to willfully misinterpret humor and whimsy as pompous self-aggrandizement and you're good to go. Just ignore the fact that, unlike most authors in this field, I don't call myself a 'Master' or 'Shifu'. Forget that I constantly tell the reader that with a bit of work he won't even need the book anymore, that anybody can experience these things, that I constantly refer to the original ancient masters as the only real authorities, and that I never make grandiose claims for my own fight skills but just say that I want to get these ideas and practices out there, as an instructor. Please totally ignore all that and seize on every minor light note or witticism as damning evidence that I'm totally full of myself. That deep psychological insight, which has nothing to do with the question of possibly useful content in the book, can be a tent pole of your 1-star review effort. Remember: the truly effective 1-star focuses on the man, not the message.

"lousy production values"

Ah! Here you're on to something good. This really isn't the kind of book you'd be proud to lay out on the credenza as the guests drift by from salon to table, is it? And considering what you've paid for this, that's the *least* you have a right to expect. Only problem with this line is that, although the photos aren't National Geographic by any stretch, they are quite good enough for straight-forward *"monkey see monkey do"* martial arts learning mode. In ancient China, the teacher demonstrated a new move only once. If you couldn't get it from that, you were stupid. And no photos. You get 'A' for effort for coming up with this though!

"he's so defensive"

Huh? Sounds kind of far-fetched to me. I can't imagine what could have given you that impression.

Well, there you have it: your paint-by-numbers guide to a *personal best* 1-star review! What's that? You say you there's more smoke than fire here? You say *what's actionable here, show me the beef*? Look, I can't write your 1-star review *for* you! Teach a man to fish. Looking over the above list, maybe I'm not contributing as much to your 1-star review as we'd both hoped at the outset. But I'm sure you can shred this book nicely all by yourself. Just beware – by reading this Appendix, you've swallowed a poison pill. This stellar tutorial on how to write a great 1-star review, all on its own, justifies at least an additional star for the book. So you're now stuck with a 2-Star baseline, just from having read up to here.

BIBLIOGRAPHY

The following works were consulted for background on Sagawa Yukiyoshi in the preparation of this book.

透明な力-不世出の武術家 佐川幸義 (文春文庫) 木村 達雄

合気修得への道-佐川幸義先生に就いた二十年 単行本 木村 達雄 (著), どう出版編集部 (編集)

秘伝日本柔術 松田隆智

孤塁の名人-合気を極めた男・佐川幸義 (文春文庫) 文庫 津本 陽 (著) -

大東流合気武術 佐川幸義 神業の合気 力を超える奇跡の技法"合気"への道標 単行本 『月刊秘伝』編集部 (編集)

武田惣角伝 大東流合気武道百十八ヵ条 単行本

石橋義久 (著)

拳児 (5) (小学館文庫) 隆智, 松田、 芳秀, 藤原

武田惣角と大東流合気柔術 改訂版 単行本

合気ニュース編集部 (編集)

新装増補版 謎の拳法を求めて （武の人・松田隆智の足跡を辿る) 単行本 松田 隆智 (著)

佐川幸義先生伝 大東流合気の真実 単行本 高橋 賢 (著)